GREAT CATCHERS

GREAT
CATCHERS

THOMAS S. OWENS

MetroBooks

MetroBooks

An Imprint of Friedman/Fairfax Publishers

© 1997 Michael Friedman Publishing Group, Inc.

Library of Congress Cataloging-in-Publication Data

Owens, Tom, 1960-
        Great catchers / Thomas S. Owens.
            p.   cm.
        Includes bibliographical references (p.   ) and index.
        ISBN 1-56799-417-2
        1. Catchers (Baseball) —United States—Biography.   I. Title.
GV865.A1094   1997
796.357'092'2—dc20   96-34656
        [B]

Editor: Stephen Slaybaugh
Art Director: Lynne Yeamans
Designers: Stan Stanski and Galen Smith
Photography Researcher: Deborah Bernhardt

Color separations by HK Scanner Arts Int'l Ltd.
Printed in Singapore by KHL Printing Co. Pte Ltd.

10   9   8   7   6   5   4   3   2   1

For bulk purchases and special sales, please contact:
Friedman/Fairfax Publishers
Attention: Sales Department
15 West 26th Street
New York, NY 10010
(212) 685-6610 FAX (212) 685-1307

Visit our website:
http://www.metrobooks.com

Dedication

To Diana Star Helmer, catcher of dreams

Acknowledgments

Score an assist for the Marshalltown Public Library Staff, who provided sincere research assistance. Additionally, without the input of those who served behind the plate, this text would be history without a heart. Thanks to all the "2s" and men in blue who care about their game.

CONTENTS

He might be called a battery mate, a receiver, a field general, or simply a backstop. But a catcher, by any other name, is still one of the most important players on the field. Ask any pitcher. Ask any hitter trying to concentrate. Moment by moment, the catcher controls the pace of an entire game.

Yet throughout baseball history catchers have usually been judged solely on their hitting abilities. Their defensive contributions tend to be blurred over time. Catchers aren't credited for assists in calling good pitches, for convincing a hurler to tough out a complete game, or for scaring potential base stealers into staying put. Imagine the new statistics possible! For now, catchers are limited statistically to gaining putouts, assists (from throwing out hitters or runners), and fielding chances accepted per game. But accepting chances is a mixed bag: catchers are often condemned on the basis of passed balls, that is, the ones that get away.

Nor do catchers get suitable recognition for the daily poundings they take. Knees and shoulders endure constant stress from constant squatting and throwing. Catchers who do their duty by blocking the plate know that the next collision could snuff out a season or even an entire career. Look up any catcher with a career of ten years or more, and check how many seasons they even appeared in 100 games. The streaks of Lou Gehrig or Cal Ripken, Jr., will never be broken by a catcher. Nothing can be taken for granted behind the plate.

Remember the 1988 movie *Bull Durham*? It's the story of an aging catcher named "Crash" Davis (played by Kevin Costner) nearing the end of his career. The team's need to have a mentor for flaky pitching prospect "Nuke" Laloosh (Tim Robbins) keeps the catcher catching for one more season.

Think it's only a movie? Think again. Each fall, as pennant races tighten, and each April, when rosters are still unsettled, the journeymen catchers begin their migration. These tireless glove men haven't stuck with one team because their spotty hitting can't justify a daily presence in the lineup. Nonetheless, their defensive handiwork—and rare ability to stay healthy—attract needy new employers year after year. Catching zombies arise from the baseball graveyard whenever a team can't stay healthy or its pitchers are sputtering.

The baseball world was slow to recognize the importance of defensive catching. Attitudes only began to change after the advent of the All-Star Game in 1933. Surrounded by leading players from other clubs, catchers couldn't be overshadowed by their teammates or blamed for their mistakes. Two stars combined in 1941 to educate fans: Mickey Cochrane and Gabby Hartnett cowrote *How to Catch*, an instructional tome from the International Baseball School All-Star Series.

Not surprisingly, the youngest fans were the first targets of literature touting theories of what makes a good catcher. Kids needed the support: throughout time, the biggest, slowest kids playing ball on the street were the ones most likely to inherit catcher's mitts. Kids learned from adults the myths that catchers don't have to move much and that their primary purpose is to be a roadblock to scoring runners.

Consider six-foot-one-inch (185cm), 190-pound (86kg) Bruce Benedict, who caught with the Atlanta Braves from 1978 through 1989. "I was just average size for a catcher, and I think I'm just average size now," Benedict told author Mike Bryan in *Baseball Lives*. "That stigma or that label that you have to be some big bruiser, or the fat, stubby, muddy guy, or the guy who got the short straw in order to catch, those have all sort of gone by the wayside. It's a little bit more of a glamour position than it used to be."

Still, catchers often seem to view their position with some skepticism. Herold "Muddy" Ruel caught from 1915 to 1934, working more than 1,400 games with six different teams. He was behind the plate for the New York Yankees in 1920, watching helplessly when a pitch from Carl Mays dealt Cleveland Indian Ray Chapman a fatal skull fracture. Ruel is credited with coining the term "tools of ignorance" to describe catching gear.

Perhaps Ruel felt only ignorant fellows would choose a position where any single play could make them goats or greats. A pesky base stealer can make a catcher look like a helpless stooge. A potential run scorer can do the same while adding to a backstop's bruises. And every pitch brings challenges for the receiver. The ball heads toward him every time.

Chicago Cub Hank Gowdy found out how fleeting fame can be for a catcher. In the twelfth inning of the decisive game of the 1924 World Series, Washington Senator Muddy Ruel lifted a pop-up. Gowdy ripped off his mask, circled under the foul, then tripped on his mask for an error. Ruel's second chance resulted in a double, leading to his scoring the winning run. Years later, guess what was the first lesson coach Gowdy would have for young catchers chasing foul pop-ups? Throw that mask far away!

Six-year Chicago backup catcher Elvin Tappe, who retired in 1962, summed up a bygone attitude in baseball. According to Tappe, catching "used to be a defensive position. If you got a catcher who also could hit, that was great. Now, it's a power station. They put guys back there now who don't really catch that well, but hit real well.

"I don't think the catchers today work at their skills as much as we did. They're more interested in taking batting practice. We were more interested in improving our defensive skills."

Of course, today's catchers can argue that new adversities stop them from maintaining

Opposite: In this photo from August 1935, Mickey Cochrane was in the midst of his second season as Detroit manager and his last as a starting Tigers catcher. In both positions, "Black Mike" got the most out of his pitchers, winning 5 of 6 games against the Cubs in the 1935 World Series.

defensive traditions. Artificial turf and balk rules that hinder pitchers from holding runners are but two complaints. However, old-timers may marvel at the way current backstops can nurse their arms by throwing out a base runner with a throw that bounces its way to second base. A rock-hard natural surface like the 1940s Sportsman's Park in St. Louis surely would have bad-hopped the ball into center field. While debating the decades, each so-called benefit creates a new burden for catchers of any era.

Harvard baseball captain Fred Thayer adapted a fencer's mask to be used by catchers in 1877. A year later, he filed a patent on the idea. Not until the 1890s did major leaguers accept the screened-in luxury. George Wright, brother of Red Stockings founder Harry Wright, preceded the mask with a "mouth protector." His invention was a fifty-cent rubber mouth guard ("without having any disagreeable taste," a sales catalog claimed). Similar to the mouthpiece a boxer wears, the invention surely cut down on the talkativeness of catchers.

Even without today's protective aids, New York Mutuals catcher Nat Hicks started creeping closer to batters in the 1870s. Before Hicks, catchers stood far behind the hitters, fielding pitches on the bounce. Hicks paid for his fearlessness, though. "He played with his right eye almost knocked out of his head," an 1873 *New York Times* reporter assessed of a Hicks performance. "His nose and the whole right side of his face [were] swollen three times normal size."

Women got into the act of making catching a safer profession. Legend has it that the wife of Detroit Tigers catcher Charles Bennett devised a chest pad to protect her hubby during games. He wore the creation outside his jersey in 1886. While some accounts say that catchers experimented with chest protectors earlier in the decade, these image-conscious receivers tried hiding the devices beneath their uniforms to avoid razzing.

Possibly overconfident behind the seeming security of protective equipment, one chatty pio-

Herold "Muddy" Ruel's catching spanned twenty years, from 1915 through 1934. His career was highlighted by an eight-year streak of catching 100 or more games yearly (1921–1928), while leading the American League in fielding percentage twice. Debates still rage over whether he or Bill Dickey gave catching tools their label of "ignorance."

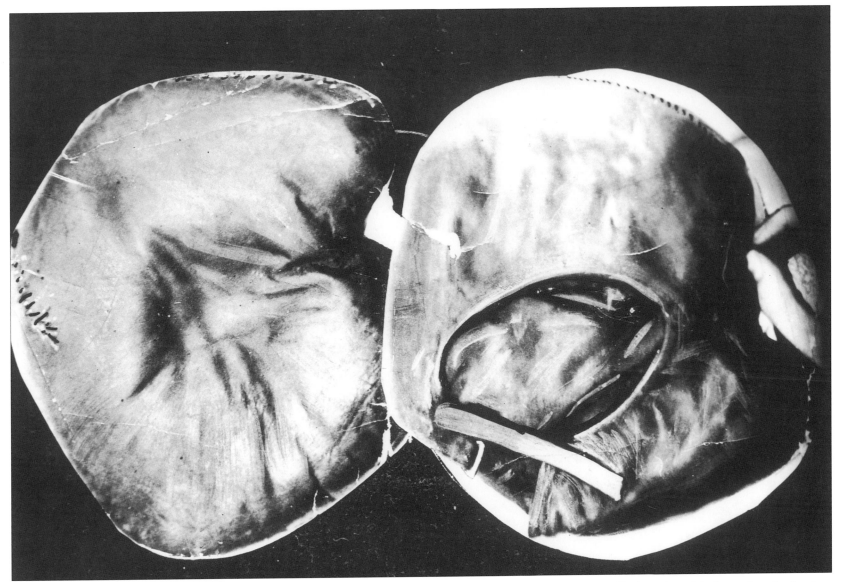

Catcher Joe Gunson introduced this mitt in 1889 to protect an injured finger. Among the many theories in baseball history regarding who created this vital piece of hardware, Gunson's involvement is mentioned most frequently.

neer helped mold the catching persona. Connie Mack, who caught for the Washington Senators and the Pittsburgh Pirates before becoming manager for the Oakland A's, got personal behind the plate. He'd annoy hitters by chatting, clapping, and even nudging their bats.

Rules were few regarding catchers. Not until 1907 were bat tappers like Mack stopped with a rule: "The base runner shall be entitled to advance one base without liability to be put out if, while the batsman, he becomes a base runner for being interfered with by the catcher in striking at a pitched ball." Before this legislation, the only guidance backstops had from the book was

the American League's 1902 ruling (based on an National League regulation from the year before) that a catcher "must stand within the lines of his position whenever the pitcher delivers the ball to the bat, and within ten feet [3m] of the home base."

Eventually, however, baseball's hierarchy found the need to limit a catcher's ability to stretch their defense to meet their schemes. A 1920 rule even dictated the terms of an intentional walk. "It shall be illegal for the catcher to leave his natural position immediately and directly back of the plate for the purpose of aiding the pitcher to intentionally give a base on balls to a batsman," sound-

ed the decree. "If the catcher shall move out of position prior to the time of the ball leaving the pitcher's hand, all runners on base shall be entitled to advance one base."

A similar rule limited the catcher's ability to control a batter. If a catcher shoved a batter out of the way during a steal of home or a squeeze bunt, or if the catcher jumped in front of the plate to take the pitch before the batter could reach it, then the hitter would be awarded first base and all runners would advance.

Mitts were a taken-for-granted part of catching, initially free from meddling rules. Historians quibble over whether Harry Decker or Joe

Gunson first used the padded catcher's mitt in the 1880s. Supposedly, Kansas City Cowboys Gunson dreamed up the mitt, but was too busy catching in Al Spalding's world baseball tour to take advantage of the idea. So, Decker filed a patent on the now-familiar mitt design in 1889. The first pro team, the 1869 Cincinnati Red Stockings, featured catcher Doug Allison and his buckskin mitt custom-made by a saddle maker. Draper and Maynard was the first company to market a glove specifically for catchers, advertising as early as 1887.

Other fielders were regulated on glove size back in 1939. But as late as 1965, baseball was still ruling on the types of mitts catchers could use.

Receivers in the 1950s had begun sporting jumbo mitts to catch knuckleball artists like Hoyt Wilhelm, cutting down on passed balls. This mitt inflation came to a head in Baltimore, when Wilhelm's manager, Paul Richards (a former catcher), unveiled a hinged-pocket mitt with a forty-five-inch (114.5cm) circumference. Finally, baseball ended the fashion fuss with a catching decree: mitts could be no more than thirty-eight inches (96.5cm) in circumference, nor more than fifteen and a half inches (39.5cm) from top to bottom. The reduction paved the way for the hinged mitt embraced by Randy Hundley and Johnny Bench.

Again, arguments flare over whether better technology makes better catchers. The newer gloves promote one-handed catching. Catchers seldom shift and move for balls out of the strike zone or in the dirt. Instead, they paw at the pitch or backhand the ball, creating more passed balls.

"The catcher is never a shortstop on ground pitches, and it is almost criminal for a catcher to try to handle such pitches only with the glove," said Branch Rickey, a famed front office executive who debuted as a part-time catcher with the 1905 Cardinals.

Yet, conversely, one-handed catching helps coerce strikes from umpires. An outside pitch can

Left: Managers Connie Mack (left) and John McGraw hammed it up before skippering the first All-Star Game in 1933. Before a half-century of managing the Philadelphia Athletics, Mack began his baseball career as a catcher. Opposite: Long before he was a manager introducing controversial catching mitts, Paul Richards was gaining experience as a receiver himself. Behind the plate for the 1943 Tigers, Richards developed an alternative to the squat. He began by resting on his left knee, with his right knee pulled in and inched to the right. He would then rotate on his left knee, using his right foot as rudder.

BASEBALL MASKS

SPRINGFIELD, MASS.

MASK WITH NECK
PROTECTING PIECE.

No. 314N. Black Enameled neck protecting mask, with two new style laced side pads, which follow the outline of the face and make a perfect fitting mask.................. $3.00

No. 313. Victor Black Enameled mask without neck extension. Made of extra heavy wire like 314N, and finished with two laced side pads............ $2.50

MASK SHOWING LACED
SIDE PADS.

No.		Each.
314	A heavy wire mask in bright finish. Has 4 laced side pads..................	$2.25
312E	A strongly made mask in black enamel finish with chin and forehead pieces. It has the regular style hair stuffed pads..................	1.75
312	A bright finish mask, slightly lighter than No. 314, and made with regular style side pads..................	1.50
AB	A high grade boys' mask, very carefully made from strong blacked wire. Has chin and forehead pieces, and good quality side pads..................	1.25
AM	A strong boy's mask in natural wire finish, with good quality side pads, chin and forehead pieces..................	1.00

NO. 312E.

No. BM. A good boys' mask, carefully made with 4 laced side pad.................. $0.75

No. CM. Youths' mask of good wire with 2 all leather continuous laced side pads.... $0.50

No. DM. A nice boys' mask with two continuous all leather pads.................. $0.25

No. A. M.

be "framed" by the catcher, with part of the mitt seen in the strike zone while catching the ball.

The catching spirit hasn't changed that much through the years. Consider the poetic musings of George Ellard, who played for the 1869 Red Stockings:

> We used no mattress on our hands,
> No cage upon our face;
> We stood right up and caught the ball,
> With courage and with grace.

Decades later, another Red Stocking would demonstrate the catching qualities of courage and grace discussed in the poem. Backstop Jimmie Wilson was the key player in this 1940 drama. Coach Bill McKechnie took Willard Hershberger out to dinner to discuss his mediocre play. This backup to Ernie Lombardi confessed that he had considered suicide. The next day, Hershberger failed to show up for an August doubleheader versus the Braves. He was found dead in his hotel room, his throat cut with a razor.

The team looked to forty-year-old coach Jimmie Wilson, a former backstop who batted only five times from 1938 to 1939. Wilson was no stranger to postseason battles. He was the top handler for the Cardinals' pennant-winning clubs of 1928, 1930, and 1931. He led National League catchers in putouts and double plays three times, topping the senior circuit in assists twice.

Pressed into action when Lombardi was hobbled by a bad ankle, Wilson did more than substitute. He hit .353 against the Tigers, recorded the only stolen bases of the 7 games, and called 2 complete game wins each from Bucky Walters and Paul Derringer. The gutsy old receiver retired for good after 1940. His leadership earned him the manager's job of the 1941 Cubs.

The future of catching will most likely be just as unpredictable as its past. But, as long as there is baseball, there will be those who love the game enough to plate themselves in athletic armor, and give home its last defense.

A page from the Victor Sporting Goods Company shows that one of baseball's first concerns of the twentieth century was to develop practical catching equipment. If you were willing to spend an extra fifty cents, Model 314N offered throat protection decades before a Dodgers catcher refined the idea. Read the product description of 312E to discover the odd stuffing used to pad this mask.

Jimmie Wilson went from being a 1933 all-star catcher for the Cardinals to becoming player-manager of the 1934 Phillies. Concluding his career with the 1940 world champion Reds, Wilson had caught 1,351 games over eighteen seasons, including a personal-best 140 with the 1929 Cards.

CHAPTER ONE

Backstop Pioneers

Catching was an art form long before Gold Gloves were presented. However, those toiling behind the plate were seen as knights in armor instead of sure-handed tacticians. Strength, stamina, and courage in collisions were the virtues most demanded.

Today, the first, best catchers are seen within a larger context. Their physical skills are appreciated in combination with their mental makeups. Each of these men became a defensive general and surrogate pitching coach while filling his role as a "2" on everyone's scorecard. (In scoring a game on a scorecard, the catcher is numbered "2"; the pitcher is numbered "1.")

Why does history remember so few great catchers from baseball's beginnings? Perhaps the lack of longevity causes forgetfulness among diamond historians. The backstops from baseball's first fifty years endured daily physical punishment, all without the luxury of today's sophisticated protective equipment. Their hitting suffered occasionally, too, playing game after game out of fear that a day off—even for an injury—could lead to unemployment.

Nevertheless, these rugged men detailed a position, and redefined a profession. Their contributions would change the face of defensive baseball forever.

WILLIAM "BUCK" EWING (1880–1897)

Credited with originating the crouching stance for catchers, William Ewing had experience at every position. Large for his day at five feet ten inches (178cm) and 188 pounds (85kg), Ewing helped cement the belief that bigger men make better catchers. While Ewing played more than 80 games a season only twice during his career, he was active in a day when catching was a grueling,

Copyright 1887. Goodwin & Co.

fill-in position that wasn't thought of as a daily, full-time spot.

Ewing amazed managers by demonstrating that he could throw out base runners while remaining in the crouch stance he helped popularize. Another innovation he circulated was a catcher's mitt modified with padding and patches. Still, Ewing reaffirmed that even the greatest catchers didn't have everlasting knees. His last full-time year behind the plate was 1890.

Beyond the plate, Ewing paced the National League in assists for three years and double plays twice. The Ohio native tied Cap Anson for most "old-timer" votes when the first Hall of Fame balloting was held in 1936. Unfortunately, Ewing wasn't around to see his pioneering catching career recognized. He died of diabetes and paralysis in 1906.

The 1919 *Reach Guide* remembered him with glowing praise: "We have always been inclined to consider Ewing in his prime as the greatest player of the game from the standpoint of supreme excellence in all departments—batting, catching, fielding, base running, throwing and baseball brains—a player without a weakness of any kind, physical, mental or temperamental."

ROGER BRESNAHAN (1897, 1900–1915)

On August 28, 1897, Roger Bresnahan debuted in the majors with the Washington Senators. The eighteen-year-old's first position was pitcher, not catcher. His knowledge of mound mechanics would help him in his second battery calling. One newspaper reviewed his pitching ability by saying that he had "a speedy shoot, an outcurve, an inshoot and a dropball."

Known as "the Duke of Tralee" for his supposed birthplace in Ireland, Bresnahan denied for years that his hometown was Toledo, Ohio (which was, in fact, the case). Judging from his tactics on the field, he could easily have been part of the

Opposite: Seen in a famous "Old Judge" tobacco card photo, Buck Ewing (right) stood tall as the sport's first full-time star catcher. **Right:** Though few believed Bresnahan's loud claims of how Irish and wise he was, no one disputed his skill with a catcher's mitt.

ROGER BRESNAHAN
Louis, National League

"fightin' Irish." He was a famed battler who faced ejections, fines, and suspensions for his ceaseless tormenting of umpires. Even John McGraw, his equally explosive manager, paid qualified tribute to Bresnahan when he said, "He was the greatest catcher I ever saw. What other catcher could hit .300, catch as Bresnahan could catch, and play any position where you needed him? What other catcher had his courage?

"If he only didn't have such a temper!"

Bresnahan first played for McGraw with the Baltimore Orioles, then followed him to New York. From 1902 to 1904 McGraw used Bresnahan mostly in the Giants outfield. But Christy Mathewson so delighted in pitching to Bresnahan that the receiving position was his exclusively beginning in 1905.

McGraw swapped the player he called "Duke" to the St. Louis Cardinals in 1908. The press deferred to Bresnahan's temperament by christening him "Rajah." When the catcher became a player-manager with his new club, the Cardinals were unofficially known as the "Rajahs," reflecting their new leader's influence. But when Helene Britton became the new owner of the Cards (inheriting the team from her uncle), newspaper writers teased baseball's first woman owner and her manager by calling the team the "Bresna-hens."

Bresnahan's contributions weren't limited to games. He is remembered as the creator of shin guards, debuting his adapted cricket equipment in a 1907 game. Incredibly, opponents, fans, and writers scoffed at Bresnahan's idea. The catcher never called himself an inventor or marketed the idea, saying the shin guards were nothing new.

Public reaction wasn't one of Bresnahan's concerns. After a beaning earlier in the decade when some New York writers actually reported his death, Bresnahan began experimenting with wearing a one-flap football helmet as a head protector. He even updated the spartan wire catcher's mask by adding leather to cushion the shock of foul tips to the face.

Bresnahan wasn't shy about his wits. He was proud to tell sportswriters about his off-season job, working as a private detective.

Bresnahan died in 1944, and was named a member of the Baseball Hall of Fame a year later.

RICK FERRELL (1929–1945, 1947)

This North Carolinian turned down a contract and a $1,000 signing bonus from St. Louis before beginning his career in the Detroit Tigers minor league system in 1926, although he would eventually play for the Cardinals from 1929 to 1933 and again from 1941 to 1943.

By 1934, Rick Ferrell was with the Boston Red Sox, a team that boasted a battery of brothers: Rick catching for his younger brother Wes. The family affair was a quick hit. The next year, Wes registered a league-leading 25–14 record. He followed in 1936 with a 20-win season.

Rick's six-year run of being named to the all-star team began with the first-ever game, in 1933. Manager Connie Mack allowed Ferrell to catch all 9 innings of the first Midseason Classic.

But on June 11, 1937, both Ferrells were traded along with Mel Almada to the Washington Senators in exchange for Ben Chapman and pitcher Bobo Newsom. Wes wasn't the toughest man to handle on the Washington pitching staff; they had as many as four knuckleballers in the starting rotation at once. In August 1938, Wes was released, breaking up the sibling combo.

Several factors stopped Rick Ferrell from getting a strong defensive reputation. For starters, the press focused on winning teams, spreading credit from player to player. And writers found that a catcher could be blamed for pitching mediocrity.

Ironically, Rick's brother had a .280 batting average—only one point lower than Rick's. Wes ended his career with a total of 38 homers, 10 more than Rick.

Upon his retirement as a player-coach with the 1947 Senators, Rick Ferrell had rewritten the AL record for most games caught with 1,805 appearances.

Approaching his eightieth birthday, Ferrell was finally honored by the Hall of Fame in 1984.

Rick Ferrell saw two tours of duty with the St. Louis Browns. His eighteen-year stint was spent entirely in the American League, rivaling Yankee Bill Dickey for the status of best catcher of the 1930s.

Owen's dropped third strike in Game Four of the 1941 Series was oversimplified as the sole cause of the Yankees championship. Umpire Bill McGowan was the first to witness the event.

Receivers and Deceivers

....

Because runs decide ball games, the spotlight shines brightest on the fielder at home plate. Throughout history, some of baseball's most memorable and mysterious plays have involved catchers.

In the fourth game of the 1941 World Series at Ebbets Field, Brooklyn Dodger Mickey Owen hatched a historic catching controversy. Dodgers reliever Hugh Casey was closing out the ninth inning, preserving a 4–3 win. With 2 outs, New York Yankee Tommy Heinrich swung and missed on a nasty curve. Unfortunately, the breaking ball squirted away from Owen. By the time he retrieved the ball, Heinrich was safe at first. The Yankees rallied for a 7–4 win, moving to a 3–1 advantage in postseason play.

Many sympathetic writers suggested that Casey had sprung a spitball, making Owen's error understandable. Yet the catcher took full blame years later, insisting it was just a curve.

Ironically, Owen was fresh from a record. From September 22, 1940, to August 29, 1941, he compiled a record-setting streak of 511 consecutive chances handled without an error.

The Detroit Tigers hosted the Yankees for a doubleheader on July 26, 1953. Detroit catcher Johnny Bucha was shaken up by rowdy base runner Billy Martin. Detroit manager Fred Hutchinson promised revenge in the second game, with Matt Batts catching.

In the third inning, Martin tried to score from second on a Phil Rizzuto single. Following orders, catcher Batts tagged Martin—flush in the nose. The bloody base runner started a bench-clearing brawl. Batts and Martin received suspensions and fines, but the tradition of catcher as defensive enforcer continued.

On October 10, 1970, the World Series between the Cincinnati Reds and Baltimore Orioles commenced in Cincinnati's Riverfront Stadium. With the score knotted at 3–all, Cincy's Ty Cline chopped a bouncer off the plate, and Bernie Carbo tried to score from third.

Baltimore catcher Elrod Hendricks tagged Carbo, but only with an empty glove, not the ball. Home plate umpire Ken Burkhart was upended in the play and caught out of position. He wrongly called Carbo out. Cincinnati lost, 4–3, on a Brooks Robinson homer.

Another Red had been involved in a catching calamity during the 1970 All-Star Game. Tied 4–4 in the twelfth inning of the Midseason

Classic at Cincinnati, local hero Pete Rose wanted to score from second on a single by Jim Hickman. Cleveland Indians catcher Ray Fosse, a rising star at age twenty-three, blocked the plate valiantly. Rose mowed Fosse down for the winning run, leaving the American Leaguer with a separated shoulder. It never completely healed, and Fosse's defensive potential was never realized.

The great Johnny Bench would be on the receiving end of a catching masterpiece in the third game of the 1972 World Series. Bench came to bat with 1 out in the top of the eighth, and runs on second and third. Oakland A's reliever Rollie Fingers took Bench to a full count. Manager Dick Williams called a mound conference.

With Bench taking his stance, Oakland catcher Gene Tenace stood, as if ready for an intentional walk. However, he returned to a squat while Fingers froze Bench with an outside-corner slider for a called third strike. Bench later claimed he was never fooled by the hint that a walk was coming, and simply couldn't hit such a perfect pitch. To save face, Bench implied that Fingers and Tenace crossed signals. Instead, approximately sixty million television viewers saw what looked like baseball's greatest fakeout. Cincinnati's consolation came in a 1–0 win.

In the 1975 World Series, the Reds would take revenge on another catcher. In the tenth inning of the third game, Cincinnati's Ed Armbrister bunted in front of home plate. Boston Red Sox backstop Carlton Fisk collided with the batter while trying to make the play. However, no interference was called. Cincinnati took a 6–5 win.

For drama, there's nothing like a matchup at home plate. And that means a catcher will always be in the middle of the action.

This photograph clearly shows that Elrod Hendricks has tagged Cincinnati's Bernie Carbo with an empty glove and that Ken Burkhart is in no position to make the call.

RAY SCHALK (1912–1929)

Ray Schalk was a 1919 Chicago White Sox starter untouched by the gambling corruption that tainted the World Series. At five feet seven inches (170cm) and 155 pounds (70kg), Schalk was far from the usual ideal of a hulking backstop.

His nimble frame helped redefine the role of a catcher. Schalk was the first to pop out of a squat and sprint to back up first base during infield plays. He became an infield rover, turning up at second base to take throws from the outfield, or covering third.

Schalk's behind-the-plate encouragement helped create 4 no-hitters, including a perfect game by Don Robertson in 1922. Fans wouldn't see another spotless effort until Don Larsen threw to Yogi Berra in the 1956 World Series. Schalk was the only catcher Eddie Cicotte ever worked with as a ChiSox pitcher. Before Cicotte was banned from baseball as part of the "Black Sox Eight," he had notched 20-win seasons in three of his last four years.

Schalk's honesty was never questioned following the 1919 Series. The next year, he became only the second man in history to catch 150 or more games in one year. Continued loyalty landed Schalk a promotion as Chicago player-manager in 1927. He retired with an eleven-year streak of 100 or more games caught yearly. When he departed, his 1,726 games caught was a career record.

Schalk became a Hall of Famer in 1955. He never spoke ill of his eight accused teammates from baseball history's darkest season.

CHARLES "GABBY" HARTNETT (1922–1941)

One of baseball's first "designated" catchers, Charles Hartnett became a regular through the endorsement of veteran pitcher Grover Cleveland Alexander.

Alexander had played semipro ball with Hartnett's father. Charles, the oldest of fourteen children, had hoped he could escape working in the Massachusetts steel mill that ruled his father's life. Fate must have wished it too, for in 1922,

Alexander demanded that the young backstop be his opening-day caddy. Although Bob O'Farrell was a capable starter, Alexander kept getting the rookie Hartnett assignments during his starts. Hartnett was the regular by 1924.

As a rookie, Hartnett was silent on the train during his first road trip. A reporter jokingly dubbed the shy newcomer "Gabby." The press had a reputation for christening Chicago Cubs catchers. A decade earlier, Chicago's Johnny Kling was considered one of the best defenders in baseball. Because of his quietness, a writer renamed him "Noisy John." But soon enough, Hartnett would earn his nickname properly. Cubs fans would remember the catcher leading the on-field charge, appearing with a whooping cry while pumping a fist in the air.

In a dozen seasons, Hartnett caught 100 or more games. But his career was threatened in 1929 when, without a diagnosed cause, Hartnett's throwing arm went limp, and he worked only 1 game. Years later, teammate Woody English would claim that Hartnett had been shooting clay pigeons, and the gun's recoil had hurt his arm. The Cubs didn't want the media to know Hartnett's true injury, English added. Mysteriously recovered in 1930, Hartnett became the National League's statistical leader in fielding.

In 1934, Hartnett received Carl Hubbell in the All-Star Game, calling the pitches that struck out Babe Ruth, Lou Gehrig, Jimmie Foxx, Al Simmons, and Joe Cronin in order.

Hartnett's career reached new heights in 1937. He claimed records of twelve years of catching 100 or more games, and seven years of topping the National League in fielding percentage. By then, Hartnett became a master in using the "pitchout," stopping base stealers before they started. Charlie Grimm, Chicago's manager in the 1930s, depended on Hartnett to tell him when to bring in relievers.

Hartnett joined fellow Chicago catcher Schalk in Cooperstown's ranks in 1955.

Opposite: Never implicated as a co-conspirator among the 1919 "Black Sox," Ray Schalk proved his loyalty to Chicago the next year by catching an unbelievable 151 games. Right: Catcher Gabby Hartnett had played in semioblivion for eleven seasons before baseball hosted its first All-Star Game. Oddly, the six-time all-star's defensive skills and endurance improved with age. He captured the National League's MVP Award in 1935.

Some of Cochrane's finest hours behind the plate were spent performing for scant crowds ambivalent about streaky Philadelphia Athletics teams. However, by the 1929 A's-Cubs World Series, the world knew of the talent burning within "Black Mike."

Gordon "Mickey" Cochrane (1925–1937)

"Black Mike," so named for his fierce competitiveness, defied catching stereotypes. In 1923, with one semester left at Boston University, Cochrane began playing minor league ball under the false name of "Frank King" because he didn't want to ruin his amateur athletic status. In college, he was a star third baseman. Upon his pro ball debut in the Eastern Shore League, Cochrane realized the only position open with the team was catcher—a position he'd never handled before. Thus he became a catcher not by choice, but by necessity.

Cochrane turned down a chance to sign with St. Louis, who offered the Dover minor league team $1,500 for his contract. The team even offered to split the money with the catcher. But because he had a deal to become a free agent at season's end, Cochrane was confident that he'd make a more lucrative deal for himself.

After breaking in with the Philadelphia Athletics in 1925, it became apparent that Cochrane had the speed to bat leadoff. He learned the fine art of glove work from Cy Perkins, the veteran catcher who was losing his job to the better-hitting rookie. One of his first catching assignments was rookie Lefty Grove. "It was like catching bullets from a rifleman with a bad aim," Cochrane later said of the experience.

In 1926, Philadelphia brought up another catcher who couldn't beat Cochrane out of the job. Luckily, the first baseman's role was open, leading to a successful transition for Jimmie Foxx, who would remain an AL longball star for a decade.

Despite the brooding moniker, "Black Mike" was a skilled psychologist, motivating pitchers and teammates from behind the plate and off the bench. In the 1929 World Series, commissioner Kenesaw Mountain Landis warned the Athletics and Cubs in writing to refrain from bench jockeying, with stiff fines awaiting violators.

Before playing in Wrigley Field, Cochrane yelled to the Cubs bench, "Hello, sweethearts, we're going to serve tea this afternoon. Come on out and get your share."

Cochrane said that Landis, present for all Series games, went into the Philadelphia clubhouse to congratulate the winners. About Cochrane's Cub-razzing, Landis remarked uncharacteristically, "Hello, sweetheart. I came in after my tea. Will you pour?"

Detroit paid $100,000 to obtain Cochrane to start the 1933 campaign. As player-manager in 1934, Cochrane led the Tigers to an AL pennant, its first in nearly a quarter-century. In 1936, the strain of two jobs bedeviled "Black Mike." His time off that season was described by some newspapers as due to a nervous breakdown.

Cochrane's playing career ended for good on May 25, 1937. New York Yankees pitcher Bump Hadley fractured Cochrane's skull in three places with a pitch. Cochrane would remain unconscious for ten days, and then be plagued by a lifetime of constant migraines. Detroit second baseman Charlie Gehringer once said that Cochrane's beaning was so severe that the ball bounced all the way back to the mound.

In 1939, Funk and Wagnalls published *Baseball: The Fan's Game* by Mickey Cochrane. A combination autobiography and color commentary on the sport, Cochrane's book even included a glossary of baseball slang current in his day. His catching-related terms included:

Pay Station: Home plate

Pop-off, or rebel: An umpire baiter

Perhaps his most revealing definition was the verb "jockey": to reveal an opponent's private life—loudly and sarcastically—whenever possible.

Incidentally, Cochrane's book contained his idea of an all-time all-star team. Muddy Ruel and Steve O'Neill were his catching selections.

In 1947, Cochrane was elected to the Baseball Hall of Fame.

Al Lopez (1928, 1930–1947)

Given the nickname "Señor" because of his Spanish background, Alfonso Lopez began his pro career with hometown Tampa in the Florida State League in 1925. Lopez was sixteen years old at the time. During his first season, Lopez was chosen to catch Walter Johnson as a team of all-stars played a Florida exhibition. "Son, some day you're going to be a great catcher," was Johnson's fabled farewell to the teen.

Lopez had sworn off baseball at age ten after getting hit in the face with a ball. The fact that he'd been skipping school to play baseball was uncovered when his chums called an ambulance for the fallen Lopez. But Lopez forgave the sport after becoming team captain for his junior high school. Older brother Emilio played catcher for amateur teams, and encouraged Alfonso to do the same.

Lopez broke in with the Brooklyn Dodgers, playing for manager Wilbert "Robbie" Robinson. Strangely, Robbie couldn't remember his catcher's name, and called the five-foot-eleven-inch (180cm) Lopez "that little Cuban." Robinson's eccentric successor, Casey Stengel, became a close friend and supporter of Lopez. When the catcher was swapped to the Boston Braves, Stengel would rejoin him as manager.

Before Lopez was through, he had rewritten records for most career games caught overall (1,918) and in the National League (1,861). His longevity streak would survive until 1987.

In 1941, Lopez tied an NL record by going an entire season without a single passed ball.

Al Lopez gained entrance to the Hall of Fame in 1977.

ERNIE LOMBARDI (1931–1947)

Early on, Ernie Lombardi would be dubbed "Schnozz" or "Bocci," saluting his large nose and Italian heritage. In fact, some fans claimed that Lombardi's odd, six-foot-three-inch (190cm), 230-pound (104kg) frame resembled a bocci ball.

Lombardi began catching for an Oakland semipro team at the age of fifteen. He insisted on holding his bat with interlaced fingers, like a golfer. Likewise, behind the plate, Lombardi was anything but a textbook receiver. He delivered the ball back to the pitcher and around the bases throwing sidearm.

The Pirates enjoyed a rare 8–3 win against the Dodgers on July 21, 1941, in part because of this diving tag by Al Lopez making the out against former Brooklyn teammate Harold "Pee Wee" Reese.

Still, Lombardi got results. With the Oakland Oaks Pacific Coast League team in 1929, "Schnozz" caught the entire 164-game season, ringing up 95 assists. Joe Cronin, a future Hall of Famer who played against the young Lombardi, once described the catching oddity. "We laughed at the way he did things, but not at the results," Cronin recalled. "You saw him throw, so you'd try to steal second base—and you'd be out by a mile."

From his 1931 debut with Brooklyn on, Lombardi was a puzzlement. On the base paths, he was a slow-footed dinosaur. Yet, on defense, he showed rugged tendencies. He never flinched while blocking the plate against all comers. Numerous teammates and foes recalled seeing the catcher snag outside pitches bare-handed. After one year, Lombardi was part of a six-player transaction with the Cincinnati Reds. Brooklyn had Al Lopez waiting in the wings.

Lombardi is forgotten as the maestro who called Johnny Vander Meer's 2 consecutive no-hitters in 1938. The same year, he won a batting crown at .342, becoming only the second catcher in history to lead the league in hitting. The next season, Lombardi faced a spring-training contract dispute with team president Warren Giles. He camped out in the executive's Florida office until his $19,000 salary demand was met.

Although Lombardi finessed the 1939 Cincinnati pitching staff into a pennant-winning performance, the catcher became a scapegoat in the fourth game of the World Series with the Yankees. The score was deadlocked at 4–all after 9 innings.

A Joe DiMaggio single would drive in 2 runs. Charlie "King Kong" Keller bowled Lombardi over at the plate. The ball rolled away while the dazed catcher was down. DiMaggio scored all the way from first when no one backed up the plate, upping the score to a final 7–4. Newspapers unfairly branded the loss "Lombardi's Snooze."

After his career ended in 1947, Lombardi struggled to find work, eventually opening a

liquor store. He tried to commit suicide in 1953. The Giants, his final team, kindly employed him as a press box custodian from 1957 through 1963.

Lombardi's friends say he died angry, waiting for the Hall of Fame call that never came. Lombardi's 1977 death preceded his eventual Veteran's Committee induction in 1986.

JOSH GIBSON (1929–1946)

Historians have ranked Josh Gibson as the greatest Negro Leagues catcher ever, simply on the strength of his great batting prowess, installing

the man once known as "the Colored Babe Ruth" in the Hall of Fame in 1972. Some of his contemporaries considered him only above-average defensively compared to other black backstops of his day.

Other Negro Leaguers who couldn't outhit Gibson exhibited mitt magic of a higher order. Raleigh "Biz" Mackey caught from 1918 to 1947, tutoring future Brooklyn catcher Roy Campanella as a player-manager. Cum Posey, the owner of Gibson's Pittsburgh team, the Crawfords, named Mackey as catcher for his all-time all-star list.

Besides Mackey, star Negro League catchers included Bruce Petway, active from 1906 to

Opposite: Ernie Lombardi posed for this March 1938 shot at the Reds spring training camp in Tampa, Florida. His sleepy looks and huge frame masked both intelligence and agility behind the plate. Right: Although Josh Gibson may have outhit every other catcher in the Negro Leagues' existence, historians aren't convinced that he was the greatest defensive player.

1925, who threw out Ty Cobb stealing twice in one 1910 Cuba series; Larry Brown, whose career stretched from 1919 to 1949; Frank Duncan, who received from 1909 to 1928; and Bill Perkins, who played from 1928 to 1947. All men were graceful field leaders who landed managerial duties late in their careers.

Nonetheless, Gibson had impressive admirers. Former pitcher Walter Johnson, later a manager, said, "There is a catcher that any big league club would like to buy for $200,000. He catches so easily he might as well be in a rocking chair, and he throws like a bullet."

In 1927, a twenty-two-year-old center fielder known as Harold "Hooks" Tinker managed the semipro Pittsburgh Crawfords. On a sandlot all-star team, he discovered Gibson playing third base.

At age seventeen, Gibson made an unexpected debut with the Homestead Grays on July 25, 1929. Legend has it that he was plucked from the crowd to substitute for regular Grays catcher Charles Williams, who had suffered a split finger behind the plate.

Gibson faced one long, nonstop season from 1933 through 1945, catching winter ball in Venezuela, Cuba, Mexico, and Puerto Rico. In 1943, he was diagnosed with a brain tumor, but refused surgery and kept playing. Heavy drinking to cope with the illness sped Gibson's demise. He died of a stroke on January 20, 1947, only months before Jackie Robinson's Brooklyn debut.

BILL DICKEY (1928–1943, 1946)

Bill Dickey's twangy speech contrasted with his defensive sophistication. Born in Little Rock, Arkansas, he began his career in 1925, playing for Little Rock, a White Sox–owned minor league affiliate. Later, through a legal loophole, his contract was obtained by New York. He ended 1928 in a 10-game trial with the Yanks. To begin 1929, manager Miller Huggins made the newcomer his starter.

As Lou Gehrig's roommate for road trips, Dickey was the first to know about the mysterious illness afflicting the "Iron Horse." Dickey was the only teammate to play himself in the 1944 Gehrig movie biography, *Pride of the Yankees*, starring Gary Cooper.

Dickey only appeared to be a stern taskmaster in guiding New York pitching staffs. Years later, he admitted that one hurler needed no coaching. "I caught Lefty Gomez without signs. He was so nearsighted he couldn't see them," Dickey remembered. "Besides, he was likely to change his mind while winding up."

Some of Dickey's most inspirational moments were initially criticized. In 1936, he was taken to task for a mediocre performance in the World Series. Later, the team trainer admitted that Dickey had broken a bone in his wrist in September, but refused to be sidelined.

How spirited was Dickey behind the plate? After a bone-jarring collision with Washington base runner Carl Reynolds, Dickey broke Reynolds' jaw with a single punch. Accounts had it that Reynolds would have been safe easily, but saw the opportunity to send the catcher sprawling. So, Dickey went to the opposing dugout immediately after the play to deliver a fist-filled reply. An unprecedented thirty-day suspension and $1,000 fine greeted Dickey's overzealous defense.

George "Skeets" Dickey inherited some of his older brother's fielding skills as a backup catcher with the Red Sox (1935–1936) and White Sox (1941–1942, 1946–1947). Both sons credited their father, briefly a minor league catcher, for furthering their interest in the position.

Bill Dickey compiled a streak of 13 seasons with 100 or more games caught (1929–1941). Only one player in the next half-century, Johnny Bench, would equal that achievement.

Dickey's defensive influence in baseball would live on in New York for another generation. In 1949 Casey Stengel summoned Dickey to tutor his successors, Yogi Berra and Elston Howard, in the fine points of catching and calling a game.

Dickey was enshrined by the Hall of Fame in 1954. In a 1958 poll, 120 members of the Baseball Writers' Association of America considered Dickey the finest catcher in the history of the American League.

Boston's on-deck batter, Bobby Doerr, wanted a choice view of the inevitable play at the plate. Yankees catcher Bill Dickey, on a throw from Joe DiMaggio, cut down runner Johnny Pesky's attempt to score on a single by Ted Williams. The BoSox won the game, 3–1.

CHAPTER TWO

Postwar Warriors

Baseball's rules and equipment had evolved; now the catcher was accepted as an essential component to any defense.

The sport's second generation of receivers adjusted their strategies accordingly. While the catchers of the 1940s may not have been "new," they were surely improved. The old-timers had paved the way for a new breed of catcher, letting newcomers learn from the mistakes and injuries of their backstop predecessors.

Equipment styles, pitch-calling formulas, plate-blocking techniques—no element of the defensive game was being taken for granted. Various players began tinkering with their mitts, trying to alter lacing or remove padding. And the new catchers began searching for updated ways to play an old game.

WALKER COOPER (1940–1956)

An eight-time all-star, Walker Cooper was the older brother of pitcher Morton Cooper. Before the second game of the 1943 World Series between the St. Louis Cardinals and the New York Yankees in New York, news came that their father had died. Walker talked with Morton, who was scheduled as the Cardinals starting pitcher. They decided their father wouldn't want them missing the game. The result was a complete-game win, the only St. Louis victory in the five-game Series. During consecutive Cardinals World Series appearances from 1942 to 1944, Cooper was the senior circuit's annual leader in total chances per game.

In 1942, Cooper helped seal a World Series title against the Yankees. In a decisive fifth game,

New York's Joe Gordon was on second with none out. Cooper picked Gordon off second base, deflating a Yankee rally, and leading the Cardinals to a 4–2 win.

Three straight Series appearances gave Cooper instant acclaim. Some attention was unexpected, however. One postseason crowd was intrigued by a foreign object that had fallen out of Cooper's mitt. Rookie catcher and teammate Joe Garagiola claimed that Cooper used a woman's "falsie," a

breast enhancement, for extra padding. Supposedly, female fans sent him extras after the slip.

The Missouri farm boy toiled for nearly eight minor league seasons before joining the St. Louis catching corps in 1941. He suffered a broken shoulder while blocking the plate in his rookie season. Cooper missed all but 4 games in 1945 because of a stint in the navy. While still in the navy, the New York Giants purchased Cooper from St. Louis for $175,000.

Catcher Walker Cooper (right) and pitching brother Morton gave the Cardinals a noted family battery in the 1940s. The talent-rich Cards had kept Walker buried in their farm system for nearly a decade.

Perhaps navy trainers would take the credit for Cooper's increased offensive output. He batted .305 with 35 home runs and 122 RBI, as the Giants set an NL record with 221 round-trippers.

In time, however, the many years in the minors began to wear Cooper's stamina and defensive effectiveness down. His last year as a starter came with the 1952 Boston Braves. Bad knees and a weight problem eroded Cooper's catching skills. Still, he became a savvy pinch-hitter and part-time coach, ending his career in 1957 where it began, with the Cardinals.

ROY CAMPANELLA (1948–1958)

From the age of fourteen, Campanella was considered a catching prospect, both with an American Legion club and the Nicetown Giants, a black amateur team in Philadelphia.

His Negro National League career began with the Baltimore Elite Giants in 1937, at the age of fifteen. Manager Biz Mackey, considered a defensive superior to Josh Gibson by some Negro League followers, showed Campanella the defensive ropes. "Campy" dropped out of school the following year to pursue pro ball full-time.

When Campanella was approached by the Brooklyn Dodgers in October 1945, general manager Branch Rickey hinted that he'd be starting his own Negro League. Campanella spent two seasons in the minors before joining the Brooklyn roster in June 1948. With his arrival, the team's other catchers switched positions, Bruce Edwards to third base and Gil Hodges to first base for a distinguished career of his own.

During Campanella's rookie season with Brooklyn, he had a string of throwing out 12 base stealers in a row. In 1953, Campanella caught 52 consecutive games without allowing a steal.

Prior to Campanella's career-ending car accident on January 27, 1958, which left him paralyzed, he faced other physical crises. Campy had undergone surgery in 1954 after playing for weeks with a wrist broken from spring training. A nerve

Roy Campanella is shown here swinging for the Baltimore Elite Giants in 1942, the year he hit .354. As with the Dodgers, Campy played catcher for the Giants, although he pitched a complete game for them in 1945. He won the game, delivering 13 strikeouts.

injury in his thumb required another operation. Every pitch brought him nagging pain, which forced him to soak his hands in ice after games late in his career. From 1949 to 1957, he caught in at least 100 games yearly. It's estimated that he caught as many as 275 games annually in his Negro League days. Add countless year-round games during eight years of winter ball in Puerto Rico, Cuba, Mexico, and South America, and Campanella's record would dwarf Carlton Fisk's all-time games record.

When the Dodgers went to Los Angeles, the pitching staff suffered from Campanella's absence. Even mound stars like Don Drysdale and Sandy Koufax couldn't avoid 1958 tailspins. Their behind-the-plate leader was gone.

LAWRENCE "YOGI" BERRA (1946–1963, 1965)

While he was growing up in St. Louis, Yogi Berra's childhood chum and American Legion teammate was Joe Garagiola. When Joe caught, "Lawdie" (a takeoff on Berra's first name) would play the outfield. With Berra as catcher, Garagiola might pitch. In the summer of 1942, both teens tried out for the local Cardinals, in an audition supervised by then–general manager Branch Rickey. Garagiola, on the basis of his defensive ability behind the plate, landed a contract and a $500 bonus.

Berra wasn't so lucky. His squashy silhouette and scattershot throwing arm spooked Rickey. When Berra tried to squeeze the Cardinals for the same bonus his friend had received, Rickey pulled the plug on Berra's future.

Berra's Legion coach convinced New York Yankees scout Johnny Schulte to sign the youngster. Of course, Berra demanded and received the same $500 his friend Garagiola received, knowing that their Italian neighborhood in St. Louis would be comparing the two careers. As a footnote to the story, Rickey joined the Dodgers as general manager a year later. He telegraphed Berra, offering him a minor league deal too late.

After a year of class-B minor league ball in 1943, Berra enlisted in the navy as World War II wound down. Before Berra's military hitch ended in the spring of 1946, Giants manager Mel Ott tried unsuccessfully to purchase Berra's contract for $50,000.

Teammate Hank Bauer remembered years later that Berra "had such development in his thighs that he could not get down far enough to bring thigh and calf together, and so sometimes they were able to steal his signals from the enemy bench." Yet Bauer agreed that Berra's agility and quickness made up for his lack of flexibility.

As testament to his hidden mobility, Berra logged 2 unassisted double plays as a catcher, tagging hitters and base runners on bunt plays. He

Left: Before two years of minor league apprenticeship, Roy Campanella was a catching star with the Baltimore Elite Giants for nearly a decade. Opposite: Although the Senators scored a surprising 12–7 win against the Yankees on June 29, 1950, catcher Yogi Berra stopped Washington's John Ostrowski from adding to the torture.

was an eight-time AL leader in putouts. Three times apiece he'd lead the league in assists and fielding percentage.

From July 28, 1957, through May 10, 1959, Berra created what were then two records: 148 consecutive games and 950 straight chances without an error. On a more subtle level, Berra influenced other catchers. Along with backup Gus Niarhos, New York receivers were the first to loop their index fingers outside their mitts. This four-finger style created a cushion against the constant pounding of pitches.

Defense alone wasn't making Berra a mythic character. Sportswriters claimed that Berra shared Casey Stengel's gift for butchering the English language. For his part, Stengel showed articulate respect for the catcher, calling him "my assistant manager" and "Mister Berra."

Teammate Johnny Mize later said, "I was there, and never heard Berra say half of those things." On the other hand, childhood pal and catching cohort Garagiola told tales to the contrary, assuring fame for buddy Berra. Entering the broadcast booth in the 1950s, Garagiola could enliven any game with a colorful Berra yarn.

Berra himself took advantage of his public persona during games. Nearly any AL batter or umpire during his era can tell tales of the chatty Yogi. Batters curious enough to listen to Berra's babbling would lose concentration quickly, playing into the shrewd hands of the supposedly daffy catcher.

Berra's last full season as a catcher was 1959, when he worked 116. His last work was a 4-game stint for the New York Mets in 1965, catching 2 games between coaching duties. Berra was elected to the Hall of Fame in 1968.

ELSTON HOWARD (1955–1968)

Elston Howard was the first black New York Yankee, breaking their color barrier in 1955. He was a Negro Leagues star before making the majors. The Yanks paid the Kansas City Monarchs $15,000 for Howard's contract in 1950. The team liked his upbringing, as well as his talent. Howard's father was a Missouri school principal; famed scientist George Washington Carver was one of his ancestors.

He said no to thirteen different college scholarship offers in order to begin a Negro Leagues career with the St. Louis Braves in 1948. He joined the Monarchs a year later. After signing with the Yanks and working five years to make the roster, Howard would star with the Yankees' minor league affiliate in Kansas City.

Howard represented a whole new school of catchers. He became a specialist with a "hinged" mitt, which looked like a relative of a first baseman's glove. Unlike the stuffed leather mitten of the past, this pliable mitt allowed a catcher to catch with one hand. The split-rim allowed this catcher's mitt to close the thumb and pinky onto the ball, much like a regular glove. Even when catching knuckleballers, Howard stuck with his smaller, more flexible mitt.

Howard wasn't a one-hander, though. He held the rim of the glove with his bare hand. "This reminds me to keep those fingers folded so I won't catch the ball on the end of one," he once said.

"Ellie" became a master motivator with pitchers. When relief ace Ryne Duren couldn't read hand signals because of his poor eyesight, Howard found a better way. The pitch Howard wanted would be signaled by the number of crouches he'd make, an easy-to-see alternative.

The Yanks began a catching shuttle in 1960, alternating the defensively declining Berra, Johnny Blanchard, and Howard between the outfield and behind the plate. By 1962, Howard had exclusive claim to the catching job. In 1963, Howard won the league's Most Valuable Player Award. For an encore, he caught 146 games in 1964, making just 2 errors.

At Howard's peak, high praise came from another defensive great. Jim Hegan, then a New York coach, said, "Howard is now the complete

Catcher Berra's "snowcone" catch in the tip of his mitt webbing was the result of a high inside pitch from Allie Reynolds. Taking a seat to admire Berra's glove work was Washington batter Irv Noren.

Tools of the Trade

Catching has never appeared to be an easy or cushy job. Even with protective accessories, the position seems to lead the league in injuries yearly.

That's why baseball's version of building a better mousetrap starts with the man behind the plate. Safety and productivity have been the goals of a variety of catching inventions throughout the history of the game.

Three noted catching inventions have been traced to the Dodgers. One of the most ingenious has been the "Campanis Target Mitt."

As a catcher, Al Campanis played only 7 games in his major league career, all with Brooklyn in 1943. His greatest accomplishments came later as a famed judge of talent for the team at all levels of the organization, and for one brainstorm as a baseball inventor. Campanis recalls:

"At Dodgertown, Mr. Rickey placed a gymnasium mat up against one of the metal fences. The mat was painted orange in the center, then blue, then white. The young Dodger pitchers would throw a ball much like a man using a bow and arrow used in archery.

"At one nightly meeting, Mr. Rickey stated: 'Some day, someone will come up with a good idea to help a pitcher with his control!' I was a young minor league manager at that time. But, many years later, when I had become the general manager and vice president of the Los Angeles Dodgers in the 1970s, I was driving home from Dodger Stadium when I saw some workmen working on the highway. It was night, and the men wore orange reflective jackets. Immediately, the idea came to me: how about an orange reflective substance around the periphery of the catcher's mitt? I knew Harry Latina, of the Rawlings Glove Company. Harry was a glove specialist, as was his son.

"I asked his son Rollie, 'Can you make up two catchers mitts with an orange reflective band covering the periphery of the glove?' In two weeks, I had the gloves. I liked the idea, and went to get a patent attorney. He told me it cost $1,500 and he doubted that I would be granted a

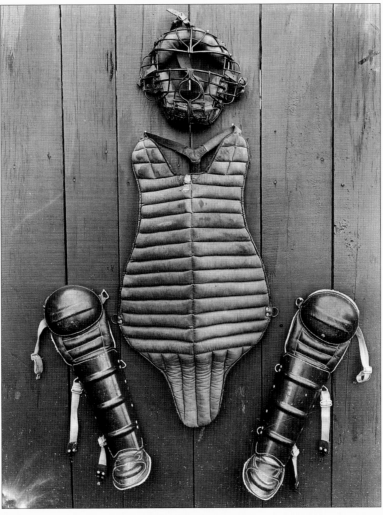

Typical catching equipment, circa 1942.

patent. I believe it only took three months. I made a deal with Rawlings. My deal was for five percent of the gross [profits] which I had go directly to my two sons Jim and George. They received royalties for many years."

Another unlikely Dodgers creator was the team trainer, Bill Buhler, who joined the Dodgers in 1957.

When Buhler was concerned about Dodgers catcher John Roseboro getting hit on the knee, he believed the knee portion of the shin guards could be doing a better job. He thought shin guards could be hinged at the knee. Unfortunately, he shared the idea with a sporting goods company representative. Roseboro got increased protection with a new shin guard, but Buhler got nothing more than a thank-you.

Of course, the new shin guards went into immediate production and have since become a tradition in the game. Although Buhler gained a bit of pride in making the game better, he never shared in any profits.

Buhler found a happier ending on September 6, 1976. He was called to action when a broken bat flew and wounded Steve Yeager, who was waiting to bat in the on-deck circle. The wooden slivers hit Yeager in the throat, almost causing a fatal injury near his jugular vein.

To keep Yeager in the Dodgers lineup, his tender, recovering throat needed special protection. Buhler rigged a shoehorn-shaped, hinged piece to hang below the chin of Yeager's catching mask. At least on defense, nothing more would harm his neck.

Yeager liked the device, but didn't receive universal praise for the contraption. He remembered Willie Stargell teasing him about the new appendage, saying "Get your tongue back in your mouth."

Buhler's first design was made out of orthoplast, the material used to make casts. One foul tip shattered Yeager's throat guard. But no one could argue that Buhler's idea didn't pinpoint a real problem and offer a workable solution. Pittsburgh's Ed Ott, Texas' Jim Sundberg, and Kansas City's Darrell Porter were the first catching contemporaries to try the improved equipment. Umpires welcomed the mask adaptation, too.

Though skeptical, sporting goods makers recognized the potential of the throat guard. Yeager's own manufacturing company agreed to mass-produce the device. Even Little League approved the throat guard design, launching sales of more than 100,000 units yearly.

Through the years, mechanical creators have failed in attempts to provide other technological benefits to the workhorses behind the plate. A noted fizzler was the bicycle seat on a spring, to be used for catchers during practice.

It seems catchers have to view inventors the same way they judge batters. While their average rate of success might seem low, history will remember the ideas that are hits, not misses.

catcher. He's a well-rounded pro who can handle pitchers, receive, throw, and hit. There's nobody in baseball even close to him today."

Howard's final hurrah came in 1967, when the Yanks tossed him to the Boston Red Sox for two pitching prospects. The veteran catcher finessed a young pitching staff into winning the pennant. Boston manager Dick Williams told a reporter: "Without Ellie we wouldn't have won the pennant. We need him behind the plate, even if he hits zero." Despite his .178 batting average, the BoSox coaxed him back for one more season. After 1968, his career .993 fielding average was the highest in history.

When asked to sum up his nonstop energy, Howard said, "I have to hustle. If I didn't, I wouldn't have it made."

Above: Elston Howard, famed as both the first black Yankee in history and the user of perhaps baseball's smallest catcher's mitt, robbed a fan of a souvenir with a foul-ball catch during a 1962 game in New York. **Opposite:** Sherm Lollar tags out Cleveland Indians Bob Avila on his attempt to come home on a single by Al Rosen in the eighth inning of the first game of a doubleheader. The effort was in vain as Cleveland went on to win both games.

SHERM LOLLAR
(1946–1963)

Sherm Lollar began his career by being in the wrong place at the wrong time. He broke in with the Cleveland Indians in 1946, a team content with Jim Hegan as a starter. Lollar was swapped to the Yankees prior to the 1947 campaign, but saw his days numbered with Yogi Berra's rise. The Yanks threw Lollar in with two other prospects and $100,000 to get established players Fred Sanford and Roy Partee from the St. Louis Browns prior to the 1949 season.

Even playing for the lowly Brownies, Lollar started drawing notice. A 1950 all-star, he led the American League with a sizzling .995 fielding average the following season. On November 27, 1951, Lollar was the centerpiece of a deal that brought five players from the Chicago White Sox in exchange for his services.

He'd win six more all-star stays with the ChiSox, leading the American League in fielding percentage five more times. He won three Gold Gloves, including the first award in 1957, when only one catcher in baseball got the honor. Lollar

Ump Bill Valentine saw action behind the plate and on the base paths. Here, he ejects Detroit pitcher Dave Wickersham following a protest at first base on October 1, 1964.

Caught on the Fly

....

What's the view like from behind the plate? Following are four perspectives

....

BILL VALENTINE
AL Umpire, 1963–1968

....

"I guess everyone has told you that Del Crandall was one of the top defensive catchers in baseball when he played for Milwaukee. Looking at his batting average, you can see he must have been, or he would not have been in a lot of line-ups. Sherm Lollar was such as a catcher for the White Sox. Both men kept the baseball in front of their body, and had quick release of the ball when runners attempted to steal.

"I liked Bob Rodgers of the California Angels. He was one of the team leaders, and he took command behind home plate. It was his game, and the pitchers threw to him. He did not allow his pitchers to argue with umpires, and would tell them that was his department. 'Just throw the ball.' [On the other hand,] Earl Battey of the Minnesota Twins was very quiet, but a leader in his actions.

"Everyone will tell you Berra ran at the mouth. But the one who ran at the mouth the most was Andy Etchebarren of the Baltimore club. He was a so-so catcher, and a real pain in the ass. He ran at the mouth for no reason, and really made his pitchers have to throw to a tighter strike zone because of his mouth. The out-of-the-strike-zone pitches he wanted when he was catching, we gave to him when he was hitting.

"Cleveland's Joe Azcue was talkative, but in a great and friendly way. Hitters would sometimes say, 'Shut up, Joe. I'm trying to hit.' He loved it when they did that, and he would keep on chatting with me about anything.

"I broke in behind the plate in the American League behind Haywood Sullivan, and he stood up so high I think I had to stand up, just to try and see around him. There was a Spanish catcher, Paul Casanova, who caught for the Washington Senators in the late sixties, who got down so low he was about knee high. That was when the big outside chest protector came in handy."

Above: Former catcher Bob Oldis served as a coach for the 1968 Minnesota Twins. Right: As a young fan, future ump Crawford watched Mickey Cochrane excel during his beginnings with the Philadelphia Athletics.

....

BOB OLDIS
Catcher, Washington Senators, 1953–1955
Pittsburgh Pirates, 1960–1963

....

"I was lucky and at the right place to spend time in the majors. Throwing out Maury Wills twice in one game in 1962, when he stole 104 bases and was only thrown out 13 times all year. I was the only guy to do that in that year.

"Ryne Duren was probably the hardest thrower I caught in AAA, and it was like a feather hitting the glove. Big Bob Veale of Pittsburgh could get it there plenty fast.

"Catchers these days keep the mask on when they throw... [back then] we threw it out of the way."

....

HENRY C. "SHAG" CRAWFORD,
NL Umpire 1956–1975

....

"Mickey Cochrane and Al Lopez were great receivers with excellent arms. The two gentlemen I mention were playing when I was a young lad attending ball games in Philadelphia. They impressed me the most. I did not see anyone to surpass them during my baseball life.

"Del Crandall impressed me the most. He was an excellent caller of pitches and was an excellent field leader.

"I must say catchers in the big leagues on the whole are not much for gabbing behind the plate. Occasionally, a joke or two may transpire between a catcher and the hitter. Usually, the hitter would be the initiator."

....

HARVEY RIEBE
Catcher, Detroit Tigers, 1942, 1947–1949

....

"The catchers I rank as defensive stars are Bill Dickey and Birdie Tebbetts. Their knowledge of hitters set them apart from others.

"These two also were outstanding at calling pitchers, and their ability to 'anticipate' enabled them to exercise great defensive moves. This also rubbed off on other players. Tebbetts would say to me, 'When you're sitting back there in that rocking chair, think about what you might do if the ball is hit to a certain area. If it's a base hit, how do you want to call pitches on the next batter to keep the runner from advancing? Some hitters are better with men on base, so you call for different pitches than with no one on base.'

"On the plate blocking, it hasn't really changed that much. No one catcher stands out in my mind. There were many good ones.

"Artificial grass is somewhat of a factor today, because the ball skips rapidly, as opposed to natural grass, on throws from the outfield. On artificial grass, some catchers skip the ball into second base to get the ball there sooner. I never had that opportunity.

"I can't recall any confrontation as such. One of the fastest runners in 1942 was George Case with the Washington Senators. He stole second on me, and me being a 'rookie,' he didn't think he had to slide. The ball hit him in the head, and he was on 'queer street' for a while. As Dizzy Dean might have said, he 'slud' often after that."

retired with a .992 fielding average, the second highest in history.

Les Moss, a ChiSox backup for Lollar, summed him up, saying, "I don't think he had an enemy in the world. He was a good, smart catcher. He should have been a big league manager."

JIM HEGAN (1942, 1946–1960)

The behind-the-plate architect of the Cleveland Indians pennants in 1948 and 1954, Jim Hegan was one of baseball's mysteries. While he dazzled baseball with his defense for more than a decade, no one could understand his lifetime .228 average.

"He wasn't a very good hitter, but he was a great, great defensive catcher, probably one of the greatest to ever come along," Elvin Tappe, a back-up catcher for the 1953–1962 Cubs, said of Hegan.

Hegan was signed by Cleveland minor league director Cy Slapnicka, who won scout immortality by signing pitcher Bob Feller. Slapnicka inked Hegan on the day the catcher graduated from high school in Lynn, Massachusetts. Unlike other kids pushed into the role, Hegan had decided to pursue catching as early as age eleven. As a signing bonus, Hegan demanded, and got, a new Packard just like the one Slapnicka drove. He idolized another catcher from Massachusetts, Mickey Cochrane.

Hegan was one of baseball's most durable catchers, with a decade-long streak of 100 or more games caught yearly. He exceeded 130 games in six of those ten seasons. Like Feller, Hegan interrupted his career in 1943, serving with the military until 1945.

The catcher was fabled for handling towering pop-ups flawlessly. "I could tell by the sound where the ball was going," he often explained. "So I'd go there and wait for it to come down."

Along with receiving 3 no-hitters in Cleveland (from Don Black, Bob Lemon, and Bob Feller), Hegan was credited with the success of assorted Cleveland pitchers. He was there for the "rookie" success of ageless Satchel Paige in 1948. Bob Lemon won 20 or more games for seven seasons while pitching to Hegan. One secret Hegan used in showcasing Cleveland pitchers was using different mitts. Although he needed a stiff mitt to handle Feller, Hegan had assorted soft, pliable mitts for other hurlers. The softer models made a popping sound as the ball hit the mit, creating an illusion of speed.

Hegan retired with a .990 career fielding percentage, with yearly averages ranging as high as

Jim Hegan hogs the plate while tagging out Boston runner Tom Wright on August 1, 1950. Hegan's heroics ensured a 6–5 win for the hosting Indians. Observe that Hegan was an old-school receiver who didn't wear a helmet in the field.

.997. *Total Baseball*'s statistics state that Hegan produced 149 lifetime "fielding runs," meaning that he saved that many runs in his career. His total surpasses all catchers of the twentieth century.

Hegan succeeded Bill Dickey as Yankees battery coach, teaching catching in the Bronx from 1960 to 1973. After coaching for the Detroit Tigers from 1974 to 1978, Hegan returned to the Yanks for two years. He died in 1984, at age sixty-three. Hegan's tutoring, like Dickey's, had an impact on many catchers, including Thurman Munson and Lance Parrish.

EARL BATTEY (1955–1967)

The opening-day catcher for the first-ever Minnesota Twins team, Earl Battey was one of the Washington Senators holdovers exported to the Land of Ten Thousand Lakes. He led all American Leaguers in fan voting for the 1965 All-Star Game and played before a home crowd in Minneapolis.

Battey's four career all-star appearances and three Gold Gloves only hint at his defensive capabilities. Although Battey debuted with the Chicago White Sox in 1955, he was trapped with Chicago as a seldom-used substitute for Sherm Lollar. Finally, in 1960, the ChiSox shipped him to Washington with Don Mincher and $150,000, in exchange for Roy Sievers.

Considering his health, Battey's seven seasons of 100 or more games caught (1960–1966) seem remarkable. His injuries ranged from two broken cheekbones and dislocated fingers to a constantly ailing knee. A goiter (from an iodine deficiency) increased his weight as much as sixty pounds (27kg). During the 1965 World Series, Battey ran into a Dodger Stadium crossbar, nearly breaking his neck. Although he kept playing, Battey could hardly speak or turn his head.

Scores of teammates praised his playing with the pain, catching with "soft hands," and being a likable fellow. "He could settle down any pitcher," Minnesota pitcher Johnny Klippstein said of Battey. "I thought he was like a granddaddy."

Twins catcher Earl Battey stopped Detroit's Norm Cash from scoring on May 6, 1962. Battey would go on to catch a career-high 147 games for Minnesota during the season.

JOHN ROSEBORO (1957–1970)

One of baseball's most underrated catching marvels of the 1960s is remembered not for defense, but offense. A different kind of offense, that is.

During a 1965 pennant showdown with the San Francisco Giants, John Roseboro wanted to teach San Francisco pitcher Juan Marichal a les-

son. "The Dominican Dandy" had thrown the ball at Giant teammate Maury Wills' knees, to retaliate for an earlier stolen base.

Sandy Koufax wasn't throwing the knockdown pitch Roseboro called. So, Roseboro decided to deliver his own warning to Marichal. When Marichal was batting, the catcher's return throws sizzled dangerously close to the hitter's ear and nose. When Marichal screamed at the catcher, Roseboro rose from a crouch to punch him.

Still holding the bat, however, Marichal held the advantage. Roseboro was hit flush in the head. Marichal knocked the catcher's mask off, getting maximum mileage from his swings. Later, Dodgers manager Walter Alston said he believed

Even as a rookie, John Roseboro wasn't shy behind the plate. In this 1957 home game, the Brooklyn catcher faced the wrath of Philadelphia's Richie Ashburn. A late relay from shortstop Charlie Neal made Roseboro's effort futile.

Roseboro's left eye was poked out with the bat because of the blood covering his face.

Roseboro's added pain came when Marichal received only an eight-day suspension and a $1,750 fine. Seven years later, a $110,000 lawsuit filed by Roseboro against the pitcher was settled out of court for $7,000.

Roseboro was a Dodger for a decade, debuting as Campanella's backup with Brooklyn in 1957. After Campy's tragic automobile accident, Roseboro was thrown into starting duty. The transition wasn't seamless. Roseboro was an outfielder at the onset of his minor league stint.

Constant effort turned Roseboro into a defensive dynamo. The "Go-Go" White Sox, who led all of baseball with 101 stolen bases in 1959, were favored to run circles around the young catcher in the World Series match-up. Roseboro allowed only 2 steals in 6 games as the (recently relocated) Los Angeles Dodgers became world champions.

Two Gold Gloves highlighted Roseboro's success behind the plate. In twenty-one World Series games and three all-star appearances, he played without a single error.

DEL CRANDALL (1949–1950, 1953–1966)

"I think the most complete catcher during my time in the league was Del Crandall," fellow catcher Roseboro wrote in his autobiography. And Crandall's time in the league preceded Roseboro by nearly a decade.

At age nineteen, Crandall premiered with the 1949 Boston Braves. He was absent from 1951 to 1952, serving a two-year army hitch in Japan. Returning in 1953, Crandall beat Walker Cooper out of a job when the team transplanted to Milwaukee. Soon, Crandall would be Braves team captain.

Crandall was a pudgy kid willing to play the position no one else wanted. He remembered promising himself from as early as fifth grade

Catcher Del Crandall hugged winning pitcher Lew Burdette after the Braves collected a Game Seven win to seal the World Series against the 1957 Yankees. Third baseman Eddie Mathews (41) joined the party. Crandall's leadership and defense would guarantee Milwaukee two straight Series nods.

that he'd make a career as a catcher. He blossomed in high school, getting contacted by scouts from all but three teams.

Prior to Roy Campanella's car accident, Crandall was relegated to second-best status. Once out of Campy's shadow, the Braves catcher began a Gold Glove collection.

Milwaukee Braves manager Fred Haney claimed publicly that Crandall was invaluable in the lineup. Crandall's worth was painfully clear in 1961, when an injured arm kept him out of all but 15 games. Joe Torre tried to fill the void, but Milwaukee sank to fourth place. Previously, a healthy Crandall had helped Milwaukee to two pennants, five second-place finishes, and one third-place finish in eight years.

Following an eight-year streak of 100 or more games caught, Crandall caught 150 of 156 games in 1959, and then 142 games in 1960. But even

Crandall couldn't keep up quality production under a massive workload forever, though. Crandall finally succumbed to injury the following season.

A six-time all-star, Crandall led the National League in assists six times. Although the leagues didn't award seperate Gold Gloves until 1958, Crandall won the award (voted on by his peers) four times in its first five years of existence.

BILL FREEHAN (1961, 1963–1976)

The Tigers reaped one of their greatest homegrown crops with Bill Freehan, a Detroit native. He starred in baseball and football at the University of Michigan before signing for a $100,000 bonus in 1961.

Freehan's first full season came in 1963. He logged 19 games at first base, while sharing catching duties with Gus Triandos. Although Triandos led AL receivers with a .998 fielding percentage, he was swapped to Philadelphia that December. Freehan responded by hitting .300 with 18 homers and 80 RBI in 1964, his first year as a starter.

Ten all-star appearances, seven as a starter, began in 1964 as well. From 1965 through 1969, Freehan would dominate Gold Glove balloting. He caught Denny McLain's 31-win season in 1968, when Detroit won a world championship. Freehan's lifetime .993 fielding mark was matched only by Elston Howard and Jim Sundberg for the best in history.

Behind the Mask was Freehan's daily account of the 1969 season. Although the book was never heralded as a locker-room tell-all similar to *Ball Four*, the biography revealed more about Freehan's career. He confessed he didn't have universal affection for every Tigers pitcher, but knew each hurler well. Freehan demonstrated that a good catcher needed to know both a hitter's and pitcher's abilities and tendencies to call the best game possible.

RANDY HUNDLEY (1964–1977)

Starting with the 1964 Giants, Randy Hundley would change the face of catching forever. He used an advanced version of the hinged glove that Elston Howard favored. The difference? Howard preferred a more traditional stance of receiving the ball. Hundley, however, could catch the ball with a squeeze while keeping his throwing hand hidden, free and away from the path of the pitch.

From 1966 to 1969, Hundley worked an unheard-of minimum of 149 games yearly behind the plate. His 160 games caught in 1968 may be one of baseball's most unbreakable records.

His 978 putouts in 1969 were more than an NL best: the stat was then the third-highest in history.

Detroit catcher Bill Freehan sent Yankee Roger Maris reeling while applying a first-inning tag. Freehan's muscle caused the shaken New Yorker to leave the 1966 game early.

Umpire Shag Crawford gave Chicago catcher Randy Hundley the benefit of the doubt in this bang-bang play from 1966. Pittsburgh's Manny Mota had tried to score. Hundley's knees wore out prematurely after excessive work for the Cubs in the sixties.

CHAPTER THREE

Home Plate Professors

Base stealing became an expected part of the game as teams fell short on power. And treating the catcher like a bowling pin in need of toppling became a scoring fad for barreling base runners.

Catchers, in turn, beefed up, conditioning like never before. Also, the advance of videotape and JUGS radar guns allowed backstops to time and perfect their throws. As a result, catchers believed they might someday be able to solve other thorny issues such as: could masks be left on while throwing? Could throws to second base be skipped across the artificial turf, getting a jump on the toughest base thieves? And most of all, was there a safer way to catch, one without suffering countless finger and hand injuries from foul tips?

Catchers became scientists, trying to devise new ways to solve old problems. As offenses became refined and stealing became commonplace, catchers needed to compete, and they knew that physical prowess alone couldn't keep a defense afloat. Catchers needed to be stronger, faster, and smarter too.

JOHNNY BENCH (1967–1983)

Growing up in Binger, Oklahoma, Johnny Bench spent many childhood hours picking cotton, working in peanut fields, and admiring the state's first great star, Mickey Mantle.

Bench's own first chance at stardom came as a fifteen-year-old in American Legion ball, competing against boys two and three years older. The first catcher's mitt he owned once belonged to Los Angeles Dodgers receiver Jeff Torborg. Torborg

gave the old mitt to a Dodgers farmhand, who was the older brother of Bench's Legion teammate. Two years later, the seventeen-year-old Bench would be a second-round draft choice playing in the Florida State League. The press showcased Bench for hailing from Oklahoma and for being part Choctaw Indian.

The Cincinnati Reds considered promoting Bench as a third-string catcher in 1966. Instead, they decided to start him with their farm team. There he began imitating Sherm Lollar from a decade before, wearing a batting helmet backward under the catcher's mask. Bench confessed years later that he devised the useful habit to control his

Right: Johnny Bench had reason to smile for this portrait, taken in Tampa, Florida, at Cincinnati spring training in March 1969. The reigning Rookie of the Year from 1968, the Oklahoma native would soon gain all-star status. Opposite: Bench greeted fans in St. Louis on July 17, 1972, scaling the fence to snare a pop foul from Joe Torre.

In addition to his stellar defensive skills, Johnny Bench had a potent bat. He led the National League in RBI in 1970, 1972, and 1974, with totals of 148, 125, and 129, respectively.

young temper. By not taking the helmet off after batting, Bench wouldn't throw (and often shatter) the headpiece following a poor outing at bat, an early practice he was often fined for.

At the end of 1966, Bench's class-A Carolina League team retired his number. One of his many accomplishments included throwing out 3 runners in 1 inning during the league's All-Star Game.

Bench debuted with Cincinnati in 1967. He started copying Randy Hundley's habit of hiding the throwing hand while catching. To aid the one-handed style, Bench broke in his mitt diagonally, making it look like a saucer. Backhanding pitches became a new trend that spread from Cincinnati. Bench's huge left hand used a catcher's mitt like

an extra skin. His large paw amazed photographers, who frequently captured Bench gripping seven baseballs with one hand.

Besides possessing huge hands, Bench boasted impeccable 20/10 vision, allowing him to pick up the spin on various breaking pitches. His heritage, his physique, and other details were bared in 1972, when Bench was featured on the cover of *Time* magazine. Although catchers had joked about their mask, shin guards, and equipment constituting the "tools of ignorance," Bench made the phrase into household words for fans.

Bench asked for a new position late in his career, when catching began taking a physical toll. In 1975, his foot was X-rayed for a suspected

break. No new injury was found, but Bench learned that he had been playing unaware of three other fractures at unknown periods prior. Near his retirement, Bench confessed that his infield style of play—making sweeping, one-handed tags—wasn't for show. Because of constant back pain, he tried to conserve movement during games.

For ten years running, Bench owned the league's Gold Glove. He also owned a senior circuit record with 100 or more games caught in 13 consecutive seasons, matched only by Bill Dickey a quarter-century earlier. "Catch You Later," Bench's trademark for autograph signings, was also the title of his 1979 autobiography. Bench took his rightful place in Cooperstown in 1989.

THURMAN MUNSON (1969–1979)

Despite defensive excellence, Munson is remembered for his life off the field. He maintained a thorough disgust for the media, and gained unwelcome headlines for defying New York Yankees owner George Steinbrenner.

Munson faced a showdown when the Yankees signed Reggie Jackson in 1977. After trying to help Jackson fit in, Munson was blindsided in a famous *Sport* magazine article. The outspoken free agent Jackson declared, "Munson thinks he can be the straw that stirs the drink, but he can only stir it bad."

All the theatrics obscured Munson's catching achievements. During his career, the Yankees team captain earned many honors: 1970 Rookie of the Year, 1976 Most Valuable Player, three consecutive Gold Gloves, and seven all-star nods.

Although his catching career was on the wane in 1979, Munson was contributing to the Yanks as a designated hitter and outfielder. He died on August 2, when the private plane he piloted crashed in his hometown of Canton, Ohio.

At Munson's funeral, former teammate Bobby Bonds described the catcher, saying, "For those who love him, no explanation is necessary, and for those who don't, none is possible."

JERRY GROTE (1963–1964, 1967–1978, 1981)

When the 1969 New York Mets performed their World Series "Miracle," Jerry Grote was getting career pitching performances out of Tom Seaver's unknown costars. Because manager Gil Hodges began his own career as a catcher, he appreciated Grote's gamesmanship.

Grote was discovered by super scout Red Murff, the same baseball guru who uncovered Nolan Ryan. "While Johnny Bench always got

Thurman Munson, shown here following the path of a pop-up, was a fine defensive player, winning three Gold Gloves from 1973–1975.

more publicity because he was a better hitter than Jerry, I will always believe Jerry was the superior catcher, thrower, and handler of pitchers," Murff (a former pitcher) insisted in his 1996 autobiography, *The Scout*. "I am not alone in that judgment."

Grote played shortstop for his San Antonio high school in the spring of 1961, but switched to catcher that season at Murff's urging. However, Grote and his father declined a $25,000 signing bonus from Houston; Grote instead began college at Trinity University, but finally agreed to sign with Murff and the Colt .45s a year later.

Grote caught 100 games in 1964, but was demoted to the minors for the following season. But Murff had moved to the Mets, and encouraged the team to claim Grote on waivers.

Grote's mitt work led the Mets back to the World Series in 1973. He became a part-time Dodger for the 1977 Dodgers pennant drive, coming off the bench to help Los Angeles to two straight postseason berths.

Although Grote led the National League in total chances per game six times, don't expect to find vintage press clippings praising his catching. After the media reported Grote blaming his manager, teammates, and umpires for subpar play early in his career, the Texan made a second career out of shunning reporters.

CARLTON FISK (1969, 1971–1993)

Carlton Fisk, from the University of New Hampshire, was the fourth player in the nation chosen in the 1967 draft. He had previously turned down a thirty-sixth-round draft offer from Baltimore in 1965 to attend college. All the while, "Pudge" couldn't shake his childhood nickname.

Likewise, Fisk couldn't escape the minor leagues. His pro career didn't start until 1968 because of military service. He got his first taste of the majors in 1969, when Red Sox manager Dick Williams let Fisk catch 1 game. The rookie was hitless in 5 at bats. In 1971, when the catching job was occupied by Duane Josephson, Fisk

Jerry Grote didn't appreciate New York's glaring media spotlight or demanding fans, but he supplied vital leadership in the 1969 "Miracle" championship.

batted .313 in a 14-game audition to win the next year's curtain call. But in 1972, Fisk was the unanimous Rookie of the Year and Gold Glove winner.

Fisk became a part of baseball lore in 1975, when his twelfth-inning homer in misty Fenway Park won the sixth game of the World Series against the Reds. Many fans may have forgotten the score or the date but still recall Fisk's body language as he motioned his hit to stay fair.

Four lengthy stays on the disabled list disrupted Fisk's progress with Boston. When healthy, though, he performed magic with his mitt. In 1977, he tied a major league mark with only 4 passed balls in 151 games. His final season with the Red Sox, 1980, featured only 3 passed balls in 131 games.

The free agent was reborn in 1981, changing from Red Sox to White Sox. He even selected 72 as a new uniform number, in tribute to his Boston premiere, though other times he told reporters that he had chosen his new number because it was the reverse of his Red Sox jersey, which was numbered 27.

To weather repeated injuries, Fisk underwent a rigorous weight training program prior to the 1985 season. He responded with career highs of 37 homers and 107 RBI. Happy with his healthy hitting, the White Sox tried to convert Fisk to the outfield the following season, but gave up after one month.

As his career wound down, Fisk did more than catch. In 1990, he passed on traditions from another era. When Deion "Prime Time" Sanders first came up with the Yankees, Fisk fumed when the "Neon" hitter refused to run out a pop fly. Without mincing words, Fisk warned the newcomer to stop mocking his opponents and the major league work ethic. Amid a fight, the future football star learned what the game meant to Fisk.

Playing in four decades, Fisk retired with a record 2,229 games caught. Though the eleven-time all-star would pace the American League in fielding average only once (.993, in 1989), his 351 homers are a lifetime best for any catcher. He was also the first catcher in modern baseball history to surpass 100 homers and 100 stolen bases.

Carlton Fisk, shown here batting for the Chicago White Sox, always seemed to have a special tie to the numbers "2" and "7;" he finished with a lifetime batting average of .270.

Masked Marvels

· ·

Sure, catching is a serious and often painful business. But some of baseball's best oddities have been born behind the plate. Here's a top ten list of "strange but true" events.

1. CATCHER CHARMS TIGERS

Charlie Bennett was a part-time catcher for the Detroit Tigers from 1881 to 1888. His career ended when he lost both legs falling under a train in Kansas.

The Tigers became an AL member in 1901 and named their new home "Bennett Park" in his honor. Until his death in 1927, Bennett was considered a Tigers "good luck charm." Moving on artificial limbs, he would precede each year's inaugural home game to catch the first pitch of the season.

2. WASHINGTON DROPS BALL

More specifically, 14 balls were dropped off the top of the Washington Monument in 1908 to Gabby Street, who was trying to snag one as a publicity stunt. The catcher succeeded on the fifteenth attempt. In 1894, catcher Pops Schriver had met success on the very first try.

In 1908, catcher Gabby Street's most memorable achievement in Washington didn't come in a ballpark. Years after his "monumental" stunt Street would become a radio favorite, announcing for the Cardinals in the 1940s.

3. A CATCHER SPEAKS

Joe Garagiola joined the St. Louis Cardinals broadcast team in 1955. After a seesaw catching career, Garagiola became an instant star by reeling off one-liners about his struggles behind the plate. Humorous tales about childhood friend Yogi Berra, a fellow catcher, increased Garagiola's following. Garagiola went national with NBC Sports in 1961, giving fans laughs and lessons about backstopping.

4. LEFTY CATCHING?

As the 1956 Chicago Cubs drained their talent pool, they summoned Dale Long to catch 2 games. Long, wearing a first baseman's mitt, became the first left-hander of the twentieth century to work behind the plate. Mike "Spanky" Squires, another lefty first baseman, subbed through 2 error-free games as catcher for the Chicago White Sox in May 1980.

5. CATCHER BAPTIZED

John Roseboro caught for the Los Angeles Dodgers from 1958 to 1967. While he doesn't cite the date of the splashdown in his biography, Roseboro claims that a home plate umpire leaned in and threw up on him behind the plate during a hot afternoon home game in Los Angeles. After that, Roseboro says he nicknamed umpire Paul Pryor "Puker."

6. ANOTHER "CAMPY" CATCHES

Kansas City Athletics team owner Charlie O. Finley made infielder Bert Campaneris earn his pay on September 9, 1965. The publicity-hungry Finley played Campaneris at all nine positions in one game, even sticking the 160-pounder (73kg) in to catch. Minnesota Twins outfielder Cesar Tovar took a repeated the "nine positions in one game" stunt on September 22, 1968.

7. RUN, CATCHER, RUN!

Cardinals receiver Tim "Buckethead" McCarver won a bit of respect for catchers everywhere in 1966. Catchers, who tend to not be very speedy, rarely stretch hits into triples. McCarver's 13 triples were an NL high, marking the first time a catcher had led a league in that department.

John Roseboro looked like a happy, dry rookie with the 1957 Brooklyn Dodgers. Years later, he would briefly turn green behind the plate.

8. O'S CATCHER CAUGHT

In a 1969 game, Baltimore Orioles catcher Clay Dalrymple appeared on the field with a fielder's glove in his back pocket. He tried, unsuccessfully, to convince umpires that he should be allowed to shed his mitt for the glove if there would be a play at the plate.

9. PHILLIES FIRST PITCH FLIES

When Philadelphia's Veterans Stadium opened on April 10, 1971, the Phillies revamped the traditional "first pitch" ceremony. Catcher Mike Ryan received his pitch dropped from a helicopter above the field.

10. OAKLAND CATCHES CATCHER

On November 5, 1978, Pittsburgh Pirates catcher Manny Sanguillen was involved in one of the strangest trades in history. Oakland A's manager Chuck Tanner was still under contract. To obtain the rights to hire Tanner, the Pirates provided Oakland owner Charlie O. Finley with Sanguillen's services and $100,000.

Giant Hal Lanier scores against Tim McCarver and the Cardinals in 1965. McCarver defied the stereotype of the slow-footed catcher, dazzling opponents with his own baserunning savvy.

BOB BOONE (1972–1990)

When he first broke in with the Philadelphia Phillies in 1972, catcher Bob Boone was known primarily as the son of Ray Boone, an infielder with the Cleveland Indians and five other teams from 1948 to 1960. In the 1990s, Bob Boone was seen as a manager, and was known as the father of second baseman Bret Boone. However, for most of the nineteen years in between, Boone challenged any team to post a more polished receiver plateside.

Boone was known for using a palm-size glove, smaller than most major league contemporaries. He broke Johnny Bench's consecutive Gold Glove streak in 1978, adding another award to his feat in 1979. His catching helped the Phils to a World Series trophy in 1980.

The coming of Keith Moreland prompted the Phils to swap Boone to the California Angels prior to the 1982 campaign. California manager Gene Mauch welcomed Boone, calling him "the best quarterback in baseball." Boone's Gold Glove–winning presence led to an instant California division title. He would win the award four more times from 1986 to 1989, the last time as a forty-year-old free agent with the Kansas City Royals.

Boone retired with an incredible 2,225 games caught, just 4 games fewer than leader Carlton Fisk. He broke Bench's and Bill Dickey's records of thirteen seasons of catching 100-plus games. Boone's 154 double plays rank fifth-best in history.

GARY CARTER (1974–1992)

Signed at age eighteen from his California high school, it was little wonder that Gary Carter's nickname became "the Kid." Carter was signed by scout Bob Zuk, who first saw him play ball at age twelve.

Right: More than his defensive talent or clutch hitting, Carter was feted for old-fashioned intensity. This intensity led him to be one of the top one hundred home run hitters of all-time. Opposite: Whether with the Phillies, Angels, or Royals, Bob Boone continued to shine defensively. His lack of Gold Gloves can be traced to sharing the limelight with Gary Carter and Carlton Fisk.

Carter started his Montreal Expos career as an outfielder, even though he was groomed as a catcher. Through Little League and prep ball, Carter had had no experience as a receiver. His catching conversion was hastened in the minors by manager Karl Kuehl, who fined Carter a quarter for each dropped ball at a time when Carter estimated he muffed 10 to 15 balls per game.

Following the 1981 season, Carter landed a seven-year contract extension that paid nearly $2 million per year.

Over his carreer, Carter proved he was one of the National League's finest defenders. Three straight Gold Gloves and eleven all-star team berths accented his accomplishments. Eight years in a row, Carter was the starting NL catcher in the All-Star Game.

After stints with the Mets, Astros, and Dodgers, Carter returned to the Expos to conclude his career in 1992. He kept catching, but resorted to a modified squat—right knee down, left leg extended—to partially salve his aching knees.

For twelve years running, Carter caught 100 or more games yearly. He retired with 2,056 games caught, a career mark exceeded only by Carlton Fisk and Bob Boone. Carter is the all-time NL leader in games caught, besting Al Lopez's NL mark of 1,861 games. Other senior circuit milestones collared by Carter include career putouts (11,759) and chances accepted (12,942).

Overshadowed by the mitt wizardry of Bench and Boone, Carter was still a five-time NL leader in assists. For six years in a row, he was tops in the league in games caught and putouts.

MIKE SCIOSCIA (1980–1992)

Although he never won a Gold Glove in his career, Mike Scioscia received unofficial honors from his contemporaries. The longtime Los Angeles Dodger was considered to be baseball's most skilled and courageous workman in blocking home plate.

Opposite: Gary "the Kid" Carter was the foundation of the 1980s Mets. His defensive stats failed to show the instrumental role he played in shaping the success of numerous New York hurlers, including one Dwight Gooden. Right: Like Carter, Mike Scioscia tried to save energy whenever possible behind the plate, modifying the traditional squatting stance that is so hard on a catcher's knees.

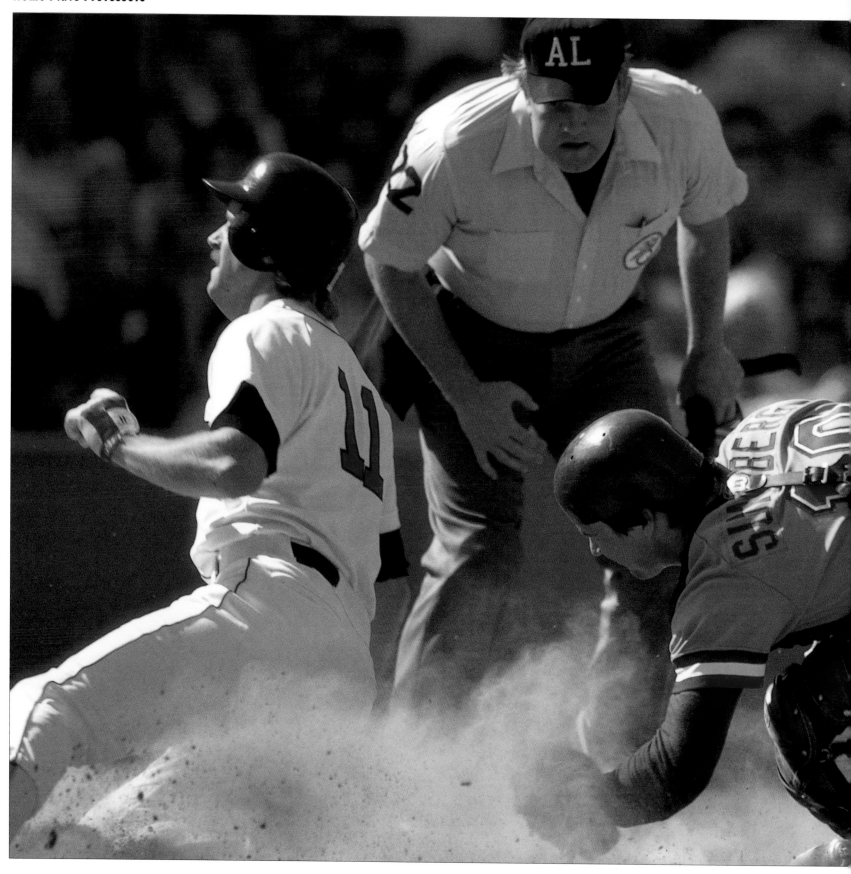

Succeeding Steve Yeager as full-time catcher for Los Angeles in 1982, Scioscia played for World Series winners in 1981 and 1988. He received the bulk of Orel Hershiser's record score-less-innings streak in 1988.

Scioscia's career faced a quickened conclusion when he tore a rotator cuff in 1983. He bounced back the next year to begin a nine-season streak of 100-plus games caught yearly.

While appearing in 117 games for the 1992 Dodgers, Scioscia knew the coming of Mike Piazza would end his Los Angeles career. Although he signed with the San Diego Padres, lingering shoulder and knee problems kept him from catching a single game. Yet another come-back with the Texas Rangers was halted in the minors, when Scioscia chose retirement.

His career highlights include ranking fourth in history in total chances and total chances accepted per game, and fifth in total putouts per game.

JIM SUNDBERG (1974–1989)

After only one year of minor league seasoning, Jim Sundberg was ready for a full-time life in the majors. As a Texas Rangers rookie, he earned an all-star roster spot. Within two years, veteran AL catchers aspired to Sundberg's defensive level. In 1976, "Sunny" began a six-year reign as the AL Gold Glove owner. Six times he would lead the league in fielding average.

Sundberg exercised contractual veto power in 1982, nixing a trade which would have sent him to Los Angeles for pitchers Burt Hooton, Dave Stewart, and Orel Hershiser, and outfielder Mark Bradley. Finally, Sundberg agreed to be swapped to the Milwaukee Brewers on December 3, 1983. One Texas newspaper paid tribute to the departing receiver, writing, "He was, in fact, something of a life preserver for Ranger fans, a hope to hold onto when there was no other."

Sundberg ranks fourth in baseball history in career games caught (1,927). He retired with a .993 fielding average, tying Bill Freehan and Elston Howard for the highest ever.

Jim Sundberg was the first Texas receiving star, setting defensive standards for catcher Ivan Rodriguez to match a decade later.

LANCE PARRISH (1977–)

Lance Parrish's conversion from minor league third baseman to catcher wasn't an overnight success. Though Parrish won the Detroit Tigers catching job from Milt May in 1979, his 21 passed balls were an AL worst.

He learned quickly. Besides eight all-star nominations, Parrish collected three consecutive Gold Gloves from 1983 to 1985. He was catcher for the World Series–winning Tigers in 1984. Going into the 1995 season as a backup Toronto Blue Jays catcher, Parrish boasted a .991 career fielding percentage, among the top ten in history.

TONY PENA (1980–)

Baseball hadn't seen many catchers the likes of Tony Pena before. The Pittsburgh Pirates catcher utilized a modified squat, in which he would fully extend his right leg while squatting on his left. At first glance, Pena appeared to be sitting in the dirt. From this seemingly contorted position, the three-time Gold Glover could snap throws to any base.

Three times (from 1984 to 1986), Pena racked up 95 to 100 assists. Mike Piazza and Benito Santiago are the only other active players who have accomplished this feat even once.

The St. Louis Cardinals gave up three starters—outfielder Andy Van Slyke, catcher Mike LaValliere, and pitcher Mike Dunne—to obtain Pena in April 1987 from the Pirates. Despite his .214 average, Pena's defense propelled the Redbirds to the World Series. When Pena began wearing eyeglasses at season's end, he became the team's leading hitter (.381 in the playoffs, .409 in the Series).

Pena's career was sidetracked after his 1989 all-star performance. St. Louis made newcomer Todd Zeile catcher, causing Pena to sign with the Boston Red Sox. When he won the Gold Glove with the 1991 BoSox, his comeback was complete. In 1994, he joined the Cleveland Indians, but caught only 40 games. His inactivity snapped a streak dating back to 1982 of 12 years of 100 or more games caught annually.

Lance Parrish was underestimated in the 1980s, both as a plate defender and hitter.

Tony Pena, here tagging out San Diego's Tim Flannery in a 1989 game, was considered washed up after being left unsigned by the 1989 Cardinals. Two years later, Pena regained fame as a defensive stalwart.

CHAPTER FOUR

The New Breed

Approaching the 1990s, baseball fans were left gawking over the departed generation of catchers. Bench, Gary Carter, Bob Boone, and Carlton Fisk took the position to "iron man" proportions. Besides hitting and fielding well, it seemed the next crop of catchers would need to excel past the age of forty to match their predecessors' statures.

Some teams began to wonder if they should sacrifice their top batsman to the daily grind of catching. The choice seemed clear to the Astros in 1991. Craig Biggio made his first all-star team while catching in 139 games, his third straight year of 100 or more games behind the plate. However, the team switched the .295 hitting Biggio to second base. A safer position, they reasoned, could guarantee years more offense from the twenty-five-year-old.

And catching casualities seemed unavoidable. The 1996 Phillies signed free agent Benito Santiago, switching longtime receiver Darren Daulton to the outfield. Daulton had been with the Phils since 1983, but didn't have enough strength in his knees to continue catching. Sure enough, he was a first-month disabled list entry in Philadelphia, admitting that years of backstop work could be the cause of his early retirement.

Nonetheless, baseball kept fielding contenders for the title of "great catcher." As the twentieth century faced the last half of its final decade, a new tough batch of catchers contended to be tops in their profession.

TERRY STEINBACH (1986–)

Terry Steinbach replaced Mickey Tettleton, who'd been released only to gain minor catching acclaim with the Baltimore Orioles, as the A's starting catcher in 1987. In 1988, Steinbach was voted the American League's starting catcher in the All-Star Game. At the time, he was battling Ron Hassey for the Oakland A's starting job, while struggling to bat above .200. However, his all-star home run won him the game's MVP honor.

Steinbach has kept improving with age. He caught Dave Stewart's 1990 no-hitter, leading "Stew" to a streak of 20-win seasons. In 1994, Steinbach's .998 fielding average ranked as the tenth highest in history.

BENITO SANTIAGO (1986–)

This catcher stunned spectators with his ability to snap lightning pickoffs without standing. In 1988, he threw out 7 runners from his knees. Even picking runners off second base was possible for the golden-armed receiver.

Yet, controversy followed Benito Santiago early in his career. He was the league's leading catcher for errors during his first two seasons. Debate flared: was the San Diego Padre bravely taking chances other catchers wouldn't, or was Santiago merely careless?

Santiago signed a two-year free agent deal with the Florida Marlins for 1993–1994. When he

Above: Joining the 1996 Phillies placed Benito Santiago with his third team in three years. Though sportswriters questioned Santiago's past attitude, his defensive reputation remained intact. Opposite: Like Gabby Hartnett years earlier, Oakland catcher Terry Steinbach achieved some of his biggest feats after a decade of experience.

was pushed out by rookie Charles Johnson, Santiago signed again with the Cincinnati Reds, coaxing the pitching staff to a division title. He put to rest the worries over his preseason elbow surgery. Ironically, Santiago had the league's highest fielding average in 1995, but lost the Gold Glove to his Marlins replacement.

SANDY ALOMAR, JR. (1990–)

Santiago's shadow obscured Sandy Alomar, Jr., for six years in the Padres minor league system. The brother of then–Toronto Blue Jays star Roberto Alomar, Sandy had done it all in AAA ball. He was the 1988 Pacific Coast League's MVP. Still, San Diego couldn't decide if Alomar should replace Santiago. Finally, the Padres made a decisive move on December 6, 1989, swapping Chris James, Carlos Baerga, and Alomar to the Cleveland Indians for Joe Carter.

Cleveland saw an instant payoff in the trade, with Alomar winning Rookie of the Year and Gold Glove honors in 1990. He was voted an all-star starter three years running.

In the years after, Alomar became a fixture on the disabled list. He began 1995 with two knee surgeries in five months, failing to catch in 100 or more games for the fourth straight year.

TOM PAGNOZZI (1987–)

"Pags" needed to be rescued from the oblivion of the St. Louis Cardinals bench. His savior was manager Joe Torre, a catcher who was reborn as a third baseman. Torre recreated his career transformation with Todd Zeile, the team's resident catching phenom.

Where could Zeile be transplanted? Like Torre two decades prior, Zeile was dispatched to third base. The opening was intended to maximize the team's defense while shoring up the hot corner.

The move, which was actually one of Torre's first acts while taking over the team in August

Sandy Alomar, Jr., displayed all the moves for the 1991 Indians, making Seattle's Pete O'Brien sweat for a score. Alomar's star fizzled in the nineties, only because constant health problems curtailed his playing time.

1990, worked. St. Louis led the National League in team fielding percentage and fewest errors for 1991. Most importantly, Tom Pagnozzi's dividends were more than defensive. He staked a permanent claim to the top job, batting a healthy .264 with 2 homers and 57 RBI, while starting 139 games. His Gold Glove credentials included apprehending 47 percent of base stealers. Torre described Pagnozzi as "the most irreplaceable player" in the lineup.

A year later, Pagnozzi gained all-star status to complement a second Gold Glove, leading the league with a .999 fielding percentage. His days of subbing for Tony Pena, then Zeile, were history.

Although he had been an infielder in high school, Pagnozzi's coach at Central Arizona Junior College suggested that he try catching for a faster trip to the majors. He was drafted by the Milwaukee Brewers in 1982, but chose to refine his receiving while getting an education through a scholarship at the University of Arkansas.

Pagnozzi was an eighth-round selection by St. Louis in the 1983 draft. He auditioned for 27 games with the 1987 Redbirds, then filled in for the team at first base, third base, and catcher for the next three years.

MIKE PIAZZA (1992–)

One of baseball's most prized catching talents of the 1990s wasn't always so revered. His career began in virtual anonymity.

Piazza garnered little attention as he played one year of ball at Miami-Dade North Community College. Previously, his experience was limited to winning most valuable player honors on his Pennsylvania high school team. He went untouched in the 1988 amateur free agent draft. Finally, the Los Angeles Dodgers chose Piazza after 60 other players, selecting him in the sixty-second round.

The catcher wasn't an ordinary Rookie of the Year in 1993. Among his first-year feats, Piazza's 35 home runs set a record for most four-baggers in a season by a rookie catcher. He threw out 58 base

Left: Nearly four years on the St. Louis bench ended for Tom Pagnozzi when catcher-turned-manager Joe Torre gave the untested hitter a full-time job in late 1990. Opposite: When Mike Piazza led the National League in hitting in early 1996, the Dodgers debated the value of converting the all-star into a first baseman. Team officials pondered how much longer the catcher's knees would survive, fearing this eventually would blight his potent bat.

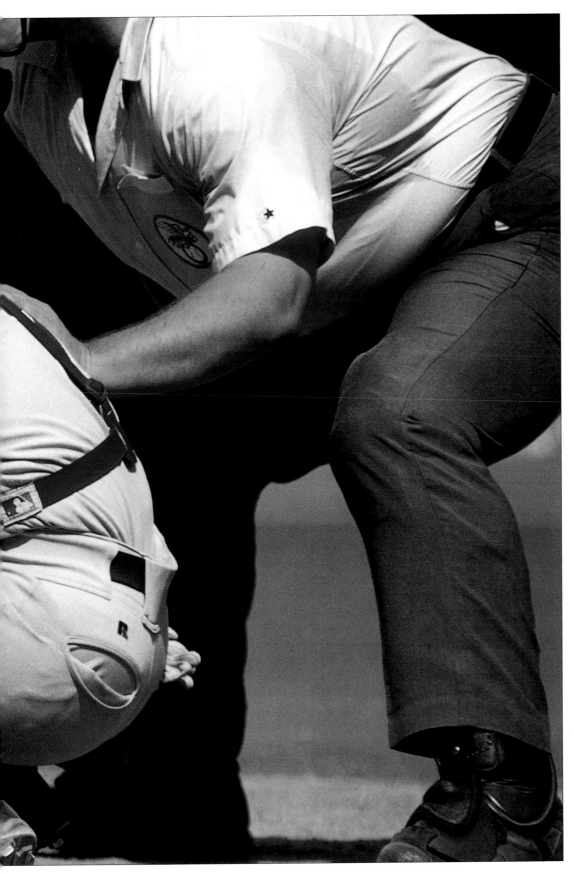

stealers, highest in the major leagues, and a new team mark.

Piazza's longevity, combined with power hitting, put him in select company. Only nine times prior in history had a catcher caught 100 or more games in a season while hitting 30 or more homers. Johnny Bench and Roy Campanella did it three times each, while Walker Cooper, Gabby Hartnett, and Gary Carter did so once. The feat would become commonplace in 1996, however, as both Benito Santiago and Terry Steinbach topped the 30-homer mark and Mets receiver Todd Hundley set a record for catchers with 41.

During his sophomore season, the league quickly showed the respect they'd learned for Piazza's arm. He gunned down 19 potential base thieves, while only 70 foes attempted to steal. Compare that to 166 confrontations during his rookie year.

When Piazza suffered a pulled hamstring to open 1995, manager Tommy Lasorda reacted in horror. "If somebody was robbing your Rolls-Royce," Lasorda defended his reaction, "wouldn't you come out of your house fast?"

Ivan Rodriguez (1991–)

"Pudge" had a big day on June 20, 1991. He was promoted to the majors, and he got married.

The Texas Rangers unveiled this catcher as a teenager. And not since nineteen-year-old Frankie Hayes caught 89 games for the 1934 Philadelphia A's had a young catcher worked so much.

As a sophomore, Ivan Rodriguez remained the youngest American Leaguer. The only younger catchers ever named to an all-star team were Minnesota Twin Butch Wynegar in 1976 and Johnny Bench in 1968 (only 11 days younger). Rodriguez was the only AL first-timer to win a Gold Glove, in 1992. Despite making a league-high 15 errors, he won the award on the strength of throwing out 51 of 104 base stealers. His 49 percent success led all of baseball.

In 1995, Rodriguez hit .303, gained a fourth straight all-star team spot, and topped the majors with a 48 percent success in gunning down stealers.

Ivan "Pudge" Rodriguez joined Texas as a teenager. His expert use of the hinged mitt has been a hallmark of the 1990s Rangers rebound.

Gold Glove Winners

....

YEAR	NATIONAL LEAGUE	AMERICAN LEAGUE
1957	(No selection)	Sherm Lollar*
1958	Del Crandall	Sherm Lollar
1959	Del Crandall	Sherm Lollar
1960	Del Crandall	Earl Battey
1961	John Roseboro	Earl Battey
1962	Del Crandall	Earl Battey
1963	John Edwards	Elston Howard
1964	John Edwards	Elston Howard
1965	Joe Torre, Braves	Bill Freehan
1966	John Roseboro	Bill Freehan
1967	Randy Hundley	Bill Freehan
1968	Johnny Bench	Bill Freehan
1969	Johnny Bench	Bill Freehan
1970	Johnny Bench	Ray Fosse
1971	Johnny Bench	Ray Fosse
1972	Johnny Bench	Carlton Fisk
1973	Johnny Bench	Thurman Munson
1974	Johnny Bench	Thurman Munson
1975	Johnny Bench	Thurman Munson
1976	Johnny Bench	Jim Sundberg
1977	Johnny Bench	Jim Sundberg
1978	Bob Boone	Jim Sundberg
1979	Bob Boone	Jim Sundberg
1980	Gary Carter	Jim Sundberg
1981	Gary Carter	Jim Sundberg
1982	Gary Carter	Bob Boone
1983	Tony Pena	Lance Parrish
1984	Tony Pena	Lance Parrish
1985	Tony Pena	Lance Parrish
1986	Jody Davis	Bob Boone
1987	Mike LaValliere	Bob Boone
1988	Benito Santiago	Bob Boone
1989	Benito Santiago	Bob Boone
1990	Benito Santiago	Sandy Alomar, Jr.
1991	Tom Pagnozzi	Tony Pena
1992	Tom Pagnozzi	Ivan Rodriguez
1993	Kirt Manwaring	Ivan Rodriguez
1994	Tom Pagnozzi	Ivan Rodriguez
1995	Charles Johnson	Ivan Rodriguez
1996	Charles Johnson	Ivan Rodriguez

*Only 1 award given for all of MLB

When Rodriguez won a Gold Glove in 1992, he became only the second catcher in history to win the award in his first full season. Although some baseball pundits wrote that Rodriguez wasn't fielding to his full potential, he remained far above the American League's defensive standards.

Honored Catchers

....

MOST VALUABLE PLAYERS

NATIONAL LEAGUE

1926—Bob O'Farrell, Cardinals

1935—Gabby Hartnett, Cubs

1938—Ernie Lombardi, Reds

1951—Roy Campanella, Dodgers

1953—Roy Campanella, Dodgers

1955—Roy Campanella, Dodgers

1970—Johnny Bench, Reds

1972—Johnny Bench, Reds

AMERICAN LEAGUE

1928—Mickey Cochrane, Athletics

1934—Mickey Cochrane, Tigers

1951—Yogi Berra, Yankees

1954—Yogi Berra, Yankees

1955—Yogi Berra, Yankees

1963—Elston Howard, Yankees

1976—Thurman Munson, Yankees

ROOKIES OF THE YEAR

1968—Johnny Bench, Reds

1970—Thurman Munson, Yankees

1971—Earl Williams, Braves

1972—Carlton Fisk, Red Sox

1987—Benito Santiago, Padres

1990—Sandy Alomar, Jr., Indians

1993—Mike Piazza, Dodgers

CATCHERS CHOSEN FOR YEARLY ALL-STAR ROSTERS

Starters are listed first followed by reserves

1933
AL: Bill Dickey; Rick Ferrell
NL: Gabby Hartnett; Jimmie Wilson

1934
AL: Mickey Cochrane; Bill Dickey; Rick Ferrell
NL: Gabby Hartnett; Al Lopez

1935
AL: Mickey Cochrane; Rick Ferrell; Rollie Hemsley
NL: Gabby Hartnett; Gus Mancuso; Jimmie Wilson

1936
AL: Bill Dickey; Rick Ferrell; Rollie Hemsley
NL: Gabby Hartnett; Ernie Lombardi

1937
AL: Bill Dickey; Rick Ferrell; Luke Sewell
NL: Ernie Lombardi; Gus Manusco

1938
AL: Bill Dickey; Rick Ferrell; Rudy York
NL: Harry Danning; Gabby Hartnett; Ernie Lombardi; Babe Phelps

1939
AL: Bill Dickey; Rollie Hemsley; Frankie Hayes
NL: Harry Danning; Ernie Lombardi; Babe Phelps

1940
AL: Bill Dickey; Frankie Hayes; Rollie Hemsley
NL: Harry Danning; Ernie Lombardi; Babe Phelps

1941
AL: Bill Dickey; Frankie Hayes; Birdie Tebbetts
NL: Harry Danning; Al Lopez; Mickey Owen

1942
AL: Bill Dickey; Birdie Tebbetts; Buddy Rosar
NL: Walker Cooper; Ernie Lombardi; Mickey Owen

1943
AL: Bill Dickey; Jake Early; Buddy Rosar
NL: Walker Cooper; Ernie Lombardi; Mickey Owen

1944
AL: Rick Ferrell; Frankie Hayes; Rollie Hemsley
NL: Walker Cooper; Ray Mueller; Mickey Owen

1945
(no game played due to wartime travel restrictions)
AL: Rick Ferrell; Frankie Hayes; Mike Tresh
NL: Ernie Lombardi; Phil Masi; Ken O'Dea

1946
AL: Bill Dickey; Buddy Rosar; Hal Wagner
NL: Walker Cooper; Ray Lamanno; Phil Masi

1947
AL: Jim Hegan; Aaron Robinson; Buddy Rosar
NL: Walker Cooper; Bruce Edwards; Phil Masi

1948
AL: Yogi Berra; Buddy Rosar; Birdie Tebbetts
NL: Walker Cooper; Phil Masi; Clyde McCullough

1949
AL: Yogi Berra; Jim Hegan; Birdie Tebbetts
NL: Roy Campanella; Walker Cooper; Andy Seminick

1950
AL: Yogi Berra; Jim Hegan; Sherm Lollar
NL: Roy Campanella; Walker Cooper

1951
AL: Yogi Berra; Jim Hegan
NL: Roy Campanella; Bruce Edwards

1952
AL: Yogi Berra; Jim Hegan
NL: Roy Campanella; Wes Westrum

1953
AL: Yogi Berra; Sammy White
NL: Roy Campanella; Del Crandall; Clyde McCullough; Del Rice; Wes Westrum

1954
AL: Yogi Berra; Sherm Lollar
NL: Smoky Burgess; Roy Campanella

1955
AL: Yogi Berra; Sherm Lollar
NL: Smoky Burgess; Roy Campanella; Del Crandall; Stan Lopata

1956
AL: Yogi Berra; Sherm Lollar
NL: Ed Bailey; Roy Campanella; Del Crandall; Stan Lopata

1957
AL: Yogi Berra; Elston Howard; Gus Triandos
NL: Ed Bailey; Hank Foiles; Hal Smith

Lance Parrish didn't match his Tigers offensive stats during a two-year stint with the Phillies. He did rise to the occasion, however, sharing NL all-star team membership with Gary Carter in 1988.

Honored Catchers

1958
AL: Yogi Berra; Elston Howard; Sherm Lollar; Gus Triandos
NL: Del Crandall; John Roseboro

1959
AL (First Game): Yogi Berra; Sherm Lollar; Gus Triandos
NL (First Game): Smoky Burgess; Hal Smith
AL (Second Game): Yogi Berra; Elston Howard; Sherm Lollar; Gus Triandos
NL (Second Game): Smoky Burgess; Del Crandall; Hal Smith

1960
AL (First Game): Yogi Berra; Elston Howard; Sherm Lollar
NL (First Game): Ed Bailey; Smoky Burgess; Del Crandall
AL (Second Game): Yogi Berra; Elston Howard; Sherm Lollar
NL (Second Game): Ed Bailey; Smoky Burgess; Del Crandall

1961
AL (First Game): Yogi Berra; Elston Howard; John Romano
NL (First Game): Smoky Burgess; John Roseboro
AL (Second Game): Yogi Berra; Elston Howard; Johnny Romano
NL (Second Game): Ed Bailey; Smoky Burgess; John Roseboro

1962
AL (First Game): Earl Battey; Yogi Berra; Elston Howard; Johnny Romano
NL (First Game): Ed Bailey; Smoky Burgess; John Roseboro

1963
AL: Earl Battey; Elston Howard
NL: Ed Bailey; Johnny Edwards; Joe Torre

1964
AL: Bill Freehan; Elston Howard
NL: Smoky Burgess; Johnny Edwards; Joe Torre

1965
AL: Earl Battey; Bill Freehan; Elston Howard
NL: Johnny Edwards; Joe Torre

1966
AL: Earl Battey; Andy Etchebarren; Bill Freehan
NL: Tom Haller; Tim McCarver; Joe Torre

1967
AL: Paul Casanova; Andy Etchebarren; Bill Freehan
NL: Tom Haller; Tim McCarver; Joe Torre

1968
AL: Joe Azcue; Bill Freehan; Duane Josephson
NL: Jerry Grote; Tom Haller

1969
AL: Bill Freehan; Ellie Rodriguez; John Roseboro
NL: Johnny Bench; Chris Cannizzaro; Randy Hundley

1970
AL: Ray Fosse; Bill Freehan; Jerry Moses
NL: Johnny Bench; Dick Dietz; Joe Torre

1971
AL: Dave Duncan; Ray Fosse; Bill Freehan; Thurman Munson
NL: Johnny Bench; Manny Sanguillen

1972
AL: Carlton Fisk; Bill Freehan; Ellie Rodriguez
NL: Johnny Bench; Manny Sanguillen; Ted Simmons

1973
AL: Carlton Fisk; Bill Freehan; Thurman Munson
NL: Johnny Bench; Ted Simmons

1974
AL: Carlton Fisk; Ed Herrmann; Thurman Munson; Darrell Porter; Jim Sundberg
NL: Johnny Bench; Jerry Grote; Ted Simmons

1975
AL: Bill Freehan; Thurman Munson; Gene Tenace
NL: Johnny Bench; Gary Carter; Manny Sanguillen

1976
AL: Carlton Fisk; Thurman Munson; Butch Wynegar
NL: Johnny Bench; Bob Boone; Steve Swisher

1977
AL: Carlton Fisk; Thurman Munson; Butch Wynegar
NL: Johnny Bench; Ted Simmons; John Stearns

1978
AL: Carlton Fisk; Thurman Munson; Darrell Porter; Jim Sundberg
NL: Johnny Bench; Bob Boone; Biff Pocoroba; Ted Simmons

1979
AL: Brian Downing; Jeff Newman; Darrell Porter
NL: Johnny Bench; Bob Boone; Gary Carter; Ted Simmons; John Stearns

1980
AL: Carlton Fisk; Lance Parrish; Darrell Porter
NL: Johnny Bench; Gary Carter; John Stearns

1981
AL: Bo Diaz; Carlton Fisk; Ted Simmons
NL: Bruce Benedict; Gary Carter; Terry Kennedy

1982
AL: Carlton Fisk; Lance Parrish
NL: Gary Carter; Tony Pena; John Stearns

1983
AL: Bob Boone; Lance Parrish; Ted Simmons
NL: Bruce Benedict; Gary Carter; Terry Kennedy

1984
AL: Dave Engle; Lance Parrish; Jim Sundberg
NL: Bob Brenly; Gary Carter; Jody Davis; Tony Pena

1985
AL: Carlton Fisk; Rich Gedman; Lance Parrish; Ernie Whitt
NL: Gary Carter; Terry Kennedy; Tony Pena; Ozzie Virgil

1986
AL: Rich Gedman; Lance Parrish
NL: Gary Carter; Jody Davis

1987
AL: Terry Kennedy; Matt Nokes
NL: Gary Carter; Bo Diaz; Ozzie Virgil

1988
AL: Tim Laudner; Terry Steinbach
NL: Gary Carter; Lance Parrish

1989
AL: Terry Steinbach; Mickey Tettleton
NL: Benito Santiago; Mike Scioscia

1990
AL: Sandy Alomar, Jr.; Lance Parrish
NL: Benito Santiago; Mike Scioscia

1991
AL: Sandy Alomar, Jr.; Carlton Fisk
NL: Craig Biggio; Benito Santiago

1992
AL: Sandy Alomar, Jr.; Ivan Rodriguez
NL: Darren Daulton; Benito Santiago

1993
AL: Ivan Rodriguez; Terry Steinbach
NL: Darren Daulton; Mike Piazza

1994
AL: Ivan Rodriguez; Mickey Tettleton
NL: Darrin Fletcher; Mike Piazza

1995
AL: Ivan Rodriguez; Mike Stanley
NL: Mike Piazza; Darren Daulton

1996
AL: Ivan Rodriguez; Sandy Alomar, Jr.; Dan Wilson
NL: Mike Piazza; Todd Hundley; Jason Kendall

When he was healthy, Sandy Alomar, Jr.'s all-star potential was hard to doubt. Instead, wishful thinkers wondered how much he could have achieved years earlier in the Padres organization if he hadn't been trapped behind Benito Santiago.

Bibliography

Bibliography

Bauer, Hank. *Championship Baseball*. New York: Doubleday, 1968.

Bench, Johnny, and William Brashler. *Catch You Later: The Autobiography of Johnny Bench*. New York: Harper and Row, 1979.

Bryan, Mike. *Baseball Lives: Men and Women of the Game Talk about Their Jobs, Their Lives, and the National Pastime*. New York: Fawcett Columbine, 1990.

Carter, Gary, and Ken Abraham. *The Gamer*. Dallas: Word Publishing, 1993.

Cochrane, Mickey. *Baseball: The Fan's Game*. New York: Funk & Wagnall's, 1939.

Falkner, David. *Nine Sides of the Diamond: Baseball's Great Glove Men on the Fine Art of Defense*. New York: Times Books/Random House, 1990.

Freehan, Bill. *Behind the Mask: A Baseball Diary*. New York: Popular Library, 1970.

Garagiola, Joe. *It's Anybody's Ballgame*. Chicago: Contemporary Books, 1988.

Gutman, Dan. *Banana Bats and Ding-Dong Balls: A Century of Unique Baseball Inventions*. New York: Macmillan, 1995.

Hirshberg, Al. *Baseball's Greatest Catchers*. New York: G.P. Putnam's Sons, 1966.

Howard, Elston. *Catching*. New York: Viking Press, 1966.

James, Bill. *The Bill James Historical Baseball Abstract*. New York: Villard Books, 1988.

Kaplan, Jim. *The Fielders*. Alexandria, VA: Redefinition, Inc., 1989.

Owens, Tom. *Greatest Baseball Players of All Time*. Lincolnwood, Illinois: Publications International Ltd., 1990.

Peary, Danny, ed. *We Played the Game*. New York: Hyperion, 1994.

Rogers, Phil. *The Impossible Takes a Little Longer: The Texas Rangers From Pretenders to Contenders*. Dallas: Taylor Publishing, 1990.

Roseboro, John, and Bill Libby. *Glory Days with the Dodgers, and Other Days with Others*. New York: Atheneum, 1978.

Shapiro, Milton J. *Heroes behind the Mask: America's Greatest Catchers*. New York: Messner/Simon & Schuster, 1968.

Shatzkin, Mike, ed. *The Ballplayers*. New York: Arbor House/Morrow, 1990.

Index

Index

Photography Credits

Jacket Photography:
Front cover: Sports Photo Masters/©Don Smith
Back cover: AP/Wide World Photos

AP/Wide World Photos: 9, 15, 20, 23, 28, 33, 41 top, 44 all, 48, 49, 54 bottom, 63

Corbis-Bettman: 14

Focus on Sports: 2, 50, 60–61, 64, 73; ©John Cordes: 62; ©Jerry Wachter: 56; ©Michael Ponzini: 75

©John Klein: 69

National Baseball Hall of Fame, Cooperstown, NY: 6–7, 10, 11, 12, 16, 17, 18–19, 22, 24–25, 29

©Fred Roe: 52

Sportschrome: ©Louis Raynor: 53; ©Robert Tringall: 70–71

Sports Photo Masters: ©Mitchell Reibel: 51, 58, 59, 65, 68, 77

©Dave Stock: 57

UPI/Corbis-Bettman: 13, 21, 26–27, 30–31, 32, 34, 35, 36, 37, 38, 38–39, 40, 41 bottom, 42, 43, 45, 46, 47, 54 top, 55, 66–67